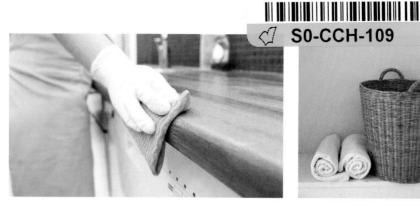

Household Hacks

Clean · Declutter · Organize

pil

Publications International, Ltd.

Contents

Introduction

You watch in dismay as a visitor's glass of wine tips over and spills onto your freshly-vacuumed carpet. You finally have time to clean your bathroom, only to discover that you're out of toilet-bowl cleanser. You don't quite know how to deal with a musty-smelling closet, but you do know it's just going to get worse if you don't do something.

We've all been there. *Household Hacks* includes hundreds of hacks to help you clean and maintain your home, cheaply and effectively. You'll find tips for stain removal when something gets spilled on carpet or clothing, guides for using everyday pantry products like vinegar, baking soda, and lemon juice as inexpensive cleaning solutions, and organizational tips that will make it easier to keep things neat and tidy. Learn how to keep your knickknacks polished and shiny, your upholstery fresh, and your kitchen and your bathroom odor-free.

Between long hours at work, family commitments, hobbies, and time spent with friends, we're kept busy pretty much all day, every day. It's easy to neglect our home while dust, clutter, and dirt accumulate. Cleaning and maintaining our household, though, helps make it in a soothing refuge when we need it most. This book will teach you ways to spend less time, less energy, and less money on your household tasks.

Cleaning Strategies

Make It Routine

- Even people who aren't ordinarily procrastinators can find it easy to put off household tasks while they pile up. Then one day we look around, and the work seems almost insurmountable, leading us to put it off for just one more day!

- By cleaning a little bit each day, and making that habit a part of your daily routine, you can make the task of household maintenance less daunting.

- Your cleaning schedule for both regular and seasonal care should be organized in a way that makes you comfortable: You may choose to clean for an hour every morning, two hours after work, or all Saturday morning. As long as you have a schedule that leaves room for spontaneity, you'll stay ahead of housework.

- Basic day-to-day chores, such as beds, dishes, baths, laundry, and floor care, require a firm routine. Big tasks, such as closets, ovens, and silver, are often best tackled on impulse and require an elastic plan. If a big chore is hanging over your head and you keep putting it off, wait. It will be there when you are up to it, and you'll probably do a better job if you are ready to tackle it. Remember that when you are in the mood to clean, your cleaning tasks will get done much faster if there are no interruptions.

A General Plan

Here is a general plan for cleaning a home. We hope you'll use it as a starting point for making your own cleaning strategy.

EVERY DAY

- Remove litter from carpets and hard-surface floors.
- Wash dishes, and wipe countertops and cooking appliances.
- Empty kitchen garbage containers.
- Wipe basins and bathtubs.
- Make beds and straighten rooms.

AS NEEDED

- Vacuum carpets and hard-surface floors thoroughly.
- Vacuum upholstery and drapes with the upholstery tool and use the crevice tool in the seams of furniture coverings.
- Dust and/or polish furniture.
- Clean the range and wipe out the refrigerator.
- Wash kitchen and bathroom floors.
- Clean toilets, fixtures, and bathroom mirrors.
- Change bed linens.
- Empty wastepaper baskets.

SEASONAL

- Surface-clean rugs and carpets, using a carpet-cleaning solution or an absorbent powder.
- Remove old wax, apply new wax, and buff hard-surface floors.
- Wash throw rugs.
- Shampoo upholstered furniture.
- Wash lamp shades, walls, and woodwork.
- Dust books, pictures, and lamps.
- Clean mirrors, TVs, picture frames, and art objects.

- Clean ovens, microwave, refrigerator, freezer, and other appliances.

- Wash bathroom carpeting and shower curtain.

- Organize closets.

- Turn mattresses, wash pads and pillow covers, and air or wash pillows.

- Clean screens and wash windows.

YEARLY

- Vacuum rug pads and the backs of rugs.

- Shampoo carpets, clean rugs, and turn rugs to equalize wear.

- Wash curtains, blinds, and shades, and clean draperies.

- Clean closets and cabinets.

- Wash or dry-clean bedspreads, blankets, and slipcovers.

- Clean out the garage, basement, and workshop.

In a Rush

The phone rings; it's a friend from school in town for a meeting or one of your mother's cousins who happens to be in the neighborhood. The surprise visitor will be at your door in 10 minutes, and your home must be ready to go on show. The following whirlwind routine will help you present a neat facade:

- Gather everything that is sitting where it doesn't belong in the entry and living areas, and dump it all into an empty laundry basket. Hide the filled basket in a closet.

- Stack newspapers and magazines on the coffee table or floor, and plump the furniture pillows.

- Give the bathroom sink and toilet a once-over, and straighten the rug and towels. Shine the mirror with tissue, and shove scattered items back into the medicine cabinet.

- Rinse the dishes, and stack them neatly in the kitchen sink or put them in the dishwasher. Wipe the countertops.

- Close the doors to rooms you don't want to display.

- Try to relax.

Tools of the Trade

A well-stocked cleaning center is the hurried housecleaner's best friend. You will be more likely to start your cleaning chores and to finish the task if you have everything you need on hand and in one place. A cleaning closet will save you time and steps; it is the efficient beginning to all the quick and easy cleaning methods in this book. You may not need everything that's listed here, but as you read this section, think about the cleaning tasks you perform regularly and stock your cleaning closet with the tools that will help you accomplish them most efficiently and quickly.

Before you supply your cleaning closet, make sure the closet has a place to store all the cleaning tools and products you buy. If you can't fit them all into one orderly place, you'll waste time digging around under the sink for the cleanser and going out to the garage for your mop. Put up pegboard or hooks to hang brushes and mops. They'll not only be easier to lay your hands on, but they'll last longer if they are hung. Install plenty of shelves to hold bottles and cartons. This will get dangerous cleaning products out of the reach of children and give you space to store a full battery of cleaning supplies, so that when you find time to clean, everything you need will be handy.

- Baskets are used for carrying supplies from one room to another and for collecting dishes you want to take to the kitchen to wash, the collectibles you want to polish, and/or the toys the kids left in the family room.

- Brushes are available in an assortment of sizes: a hard-bristled scrub brush, toilet brushes (one for each bathroom), a radiator brush, and other soft- and medium-bristled brushes for scrubbing and dusting.

- Buckets with double compartments hold both your cleaning solution and rinse water.

- Cleaning cloths are made from worn-out clothes, sheets, and towels. Cotton or linen, white or light-colored fabrics are best.

- Mops should have detachable heads for easy cleaning.

- Stepladders, at least three feet tall, are a safe substitute for the unsteady chair.

- Rubber gloves only protect your hands if you wear them. Don't forget to put yours on whenever you work with cleaning solutions.

- Your vacuum cleaner with a set of cleaning tools and a small handheld vacuum are some of the most essential tools in your cleaning closet.

- A balled-up pair of pantyhose can serve as a nonscratch pad to scrub walls, windows, sinks, and bathtubs.

- Scouring pads are made of both synthetics and steel wool. Keep a variety in your cleaning closet. Sponges should be tossed out as soon as they start to shred. Have plenty on hand.

- If you run out of paper towels, coffee filters can fill in and help mop up spills.

- Old toothbrushes work well to clean combs, silverware, and tile grout.

Cleaning Your Cleaning Tools

- Clean and deodorize smelly floor mops or sponges by soaking them for 10 minutes in a gallon of water mixed with 3/4 cup bleach. Rinse thoroughly afterward.

- Eliminate residue and smells from mops or rags by soaking them in a mixture of 4 tablespoons baking soda and 1 gallon water.

- Soak a well-worn, smelly sponge in a shallow dish of vinegar for several hours. Rinse sponge well, then let dry. In humid weather, store the sponge in a shallow dish of vinegar to keep it from souring.

Cleaning Agents

In addition to your cleaning tools, you need to have on hand several basic cleaning supplies. Keep in mind that products that are tough on grime are often tough on you, especially your hands, face, and lungs. Always read product labels. When cleaning with bleach, ammonia, or borax, wear rubber gloves and keep the area well ventilated. Also, don't mix bleach with ammonia—it can produce a poisonous gas.

All-purpose cleaners remove grease and grimy dirt.

Ammonia is available in clear or sudsy form. It is an excellent cleaner or cleaning booster for many household surfaces. It is a grease cutter, wax stripper, window cleaner, and general soil remover. If you object to the strong odor of ammonia, buy a scented product, but neither scented ammonia nor sudsy ammonia is suitable for stain removal.

Baking soda is one of the most versatile cleaning products available. Used by itself in dry form, it acts as a very mild scouring powder that will not scratch even the most delicate surfaces. Add water to make a paste, and use baking soda to scour dirty surfaces. Combined with other ingredients, it makes a very good cleaning solution that also deodorizes.

Baking powder can be used to remove odors, among other applications.

Bleach helps remove stains and whiten laundry, and it's also good for cleaning toilets.

Flour is useful for some cleaning tasks. Always use flour in its dry form because it creates a gluey paste when mixed with water.

Lemon juice, either bottled or squeezed from a cut lemon, provides the mild acid reaction needed for many cleaning solutions.

Liquid dishwashing detergents can be used for many cleaning tasks in addition to doing dishes.

Salt is surprisingly versatile in helping clean, prevent messes, and remove odors.

Vinegar is also an acid; it can usually be substituted for lemon juice. White vinegar should be used to clean fabrics, but cider vinegar is adequate for most other applications.

Waxes, **polishes, and oils** shine and protect wood, leather, brass, chrome, silver, glass, and other surfaces.

Tips While You Clean

- Don't let unreachable cobwebs get you down. Wrap a tennis ball in a dust rag; secure it with a few rubber bands. Assuming the room is free of breakables, toss the ball at the webs.

- Pour a little cornstarch into your palm and rub your hands together to make rubber gloves easier to slide on and off.

- Sprinkling baking powder into rubber gloves is another way to ensure they'll come right off when your work is done.

- Put a rubber band around each spray bottle and other cleaning-product containers. Tuck a sponge or clean cloth under the band so you'll always have one at hand.

- **Windows:** Wipe horizontally on the outside and vertically on the inside, so you'll know on which side of the glass any streaks lie. Choose a cloudy day rather than a sunny one for cleaning windows: The sun dries the glass too quickly and causes streaks.

- **Walls:** Wash painted walls from the top to the bottom. This prevents water from dripping down the wall, creating hard-to-remove streaks.

- **Dusting and Vacuuming:** Clean a room by first dusting its highest surface and then working your way down. With gravity's help, dust and dirt settle down to the floor. Vacuum or sweep the floor last.

- Are your hands a mess from grease, gardening, or generally getting things done? Clean very dirty hands by scrubbing with cornmeal that has been moistened with a little bit of apple cider vinegar. Thoroughly scrub your hands. Rinse well and dry; repeat if necessary. Your hands will be soft and smooth—and the dirt will be gone!

Everything and the Kitchen Sink

Cooking is a messy task. The only way to deal with the mess in the kitchen is to control it with quick, daily cleanups.

In most households, there are cooks and there are eaters. Use this division of labor to everyone's advantage for regular kitchen maintenance. Cooks are responsible for blotting spills when they happen and getting dirty cooking utensils into the sink or dishwasher. But after dinner, the cleanup crew takes over from the cooks. Keeping the kitchen fairly clean beats having to spend regular long stretches of time cleaning it. We have dozens of hacks to help you keep your kitchen clean, sanitary, and organized.

Countertops

- Remove stains from laminate countertops with a paste of baking soda and water. Apply, let dry, then rub off and rinse.

- Use club soda to clean your kitchen counters, stovetop, and stainless-steel fixtures. Just pour it directly on a sponge and wipe clean. Rinse with warm water, then dry thoroughly.

- Wipe your kitchen countertops with undiluted distilled white vinegar once a day to shine them and keep your kitchen smelling fresh.

- Rub a piece of wax paper over your tile or laminate kitchen countertops. The shine will send you reaching for your sunglasses.

- Remove permanent marker from countertops and appliances with isopropyl rubbing alcohol.

- Clean polished marble and metal surfaces with chalk. Crush white chalk in a clear storage bag, tapping it gently with a hammer. Dip a soft cloth into the powder and rub.

- Banish stains on butcher-block countertops and wood cutting boards with regular bleach. Soak a white dishcloth in undiluted bleach. Lay it over the spots, then wait 10 to 15 minutes. Rinse with clear water.

Cutting Boards

- You can keep odors from a clean wood or plastic cutting board by wiping it with a sponge dampened with a little vinegar.

- After cleaning your wood cutting board, rub a bit of lemon juice on it to help get rid of garlic, onion, or fish smells.

- Use bleach to keep a wood cutting board free of bacteria. Wash the cutting board in hot, sudsy water and rinse thoroughly. Then mix 3 tablespoons bleach with 1 gallon warm water. Soak or brush the solution onto the cutting board, keep it moist for at least 2 minutes, then rinse thoroughly.

- Deodorize and remove stains from wood cutting boards, bowls, or utensils with a solution of 4 tablespoons baking soda to 1 quart water.

- To disinfect a plastic cutting board after it's been washed, place it in a solution of 1 tablespoon bleach per gallon of water. Soak for 2 minutes; drain and air-dry.

Sinks & Fixtures

- Remove water spots from stainless-steel appliances and fixtures using a cloth dampened with isopropyl rubbing alcohol.

- Clean stainless-steel sinks with a paste of baking soda and water, or sprinkle baking soda directly onto a sponge and scrub the surface. Rinse and buff dry.

- Mix lemon juice and salt to the consistency of toothpaste, and apply to brass, copper, or stainless-steel sinks and fixtures. Gently scrub, then rinse.

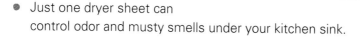

- Clean chrome fixtures by simply wiping them with plain vinegar. If the chrome is heavily spotted, wipe with a sponge dampened with vinegar and sprinkled with a little baking soda.

- Just one dryer sheet can control odor and musty smells under your kitchen sink.

Down the Drain

- Pour a strong salt solution of 1 cup salt and 2 cups hot water down the kitchen drain to eliminate odors and break up grease deposits.

- To dislodge greasy foods that may be clogging up your drain, sprinkle 1/2 cup salt and 1/2 cup baking soda into the drain. Run hot tap water to flush.

- Once a week, pour a can of Pepsi down the drain to keep it clear and unclogged.

- Baking soda and vinegar will foam your drain clean and help prevent clogs. Pour 1/2 cup baking soda down the drain, followed by 1 cup distilled white vinegar. When foam subsides, rinse with hot water. This also works well on garbage disposals.

- Clear kitchen sink drainpipes of mold- and bacteria-breeding food particles. Once a week, pour in a solution of 1 tablespoon bleach in 1 gallon water. Wait a few minutes, then flush with cold running water for several minutes.

Fridge & Freezer

- To clean and refresh the inside of your refrigerator, sprinkle equal amounts of salt and baking soda onto a damp sponge and wipe down all surfaces. Wipe clean with a fresh sponge dampened with water.

- Remove mildew spots and prevent mildew buildup inside your refrigerator by wiping occasionally with a sponge dampened in undiluted vinegar. A toothbrush is an excellent tool for reaching inside the folds of the rubber seals. No need to rinse afterward.

- Use a clean, dry toothbrush to remove crumbs and crud from the seals around refrigerator and freezer doors.

- Place a sheet of aluminum foil on the floor of your freezer to keep spills and ice cube trays from sticking. Be sure not to cover any vents or other openings.

- Trying to vacuum under the refrigerator or another hard-to-reach spot? Put a cardboard tube from a roll of paper towels, gift wrap, or another product on the end of the hose attachment. For narrow openings, bend or flatten the tube.

- Don't waste a ruined pair of pantyhose—use it to clean under your refrigerator. Wrap the nylon around a yardstick, then run it under the refrigerator.

- To remove any unpleasant taste in ice cubes from an automatic ice cube maker, clean the removable parts of the unit with baking soda and water.

Oven & Stovetop

- Spills on stovetops and in ovens are no match for this mixture: Make a paste of lemon juice, water, and baking soda. Apply to spills, let sit 15 minutes, then scrub and rinse with water and a sponge.

- Stovetop spills can be cleaned up easily if first sprinkled with salt. The mildly abrasive quality of salt removes stuck-on food, but it won't mar your stove's surface.

- Clean burned-on food from a stovetop burner by sprinkling it with a mixture of salt and ground cinnamon, then wiping away immediately. The mixture will give off a pleasant smell and cover up any burnt odor the next time you turn on the burner.

- Soak up liquid spills on stovetop burners in much the same way, sprinkling with a mixture of salt and ground cinnamon. Leave mixture on spill for 5 minutes to absorb liquid, then wipe away.

- To prevent grease splatters from sticking to the wall behind your stove, spray a painted or wallpapered wall with furniture polish and buff it with a soft cloth.

- Make your oven practically self-cleaning! In a glass baking dish, mix 2 cups warm water and 1/4 cup ammonia. Place it in the oven, shut the door, and let it work overnight. The next morning, sprinkle oven with baking soda and wipe clean with a damp sponge...and no elbow grease.

- Combine equal parts vinegar and hot water in a small bowl. Use this solution and a sponge to rub away any dried-on stains in your oven and help prevent grease buildup.

- Eliminate the odor from a commercial oven cleaner with a solution of 2 cups vinegar and 3 quarts warm water. Dip a sponge into mixture and wring it well, then wipe down the inside surfaces of the oven. There's no need to rinse.

- If a pie or similar sugary confection boils over in your oven, sprinkle the sticky spill with salt while the oven is still hot. Let it sit until spilled area becomes crisp, then lift off with a spatula when oven cools.

- Get rid of stubborn baked-on or blackened areas on an oven rack by "steaming" off the soot with ammonia vapors. Just lay the rack on an old towel in your bathtub. (Be sure the bathroom is well ventilated.) Fill the tub with warm water and 1/2 cup ammonia; let sit for half an hour. Rinse. (This also works for barbecue grill racks.)

- A similar technique for loosening burned-on foods from oven or grill racks is to place the racks in a trash bag. Mix 1 cup baking soda and 1/2 cup ammonia and pour over the racks. Close the bag and let sit overnight. Scrub and rinse well in the morning.

- Combine the following ingredients to cut grease buildup on stoves, backsplashes, or glossy enamel surfaces: 3 cups baking soda, 2 cups vinegar, 1 cup ammonia, and 1 gallon hot water. Wear rubber gloves when you wipe on the mixture, making sure room is well ventilated. Wipe clean with a damp sponge.

- Clean up a grease spatter on the kitchen wall with a bit of cornstarch on a paper towel or soft cloth. Gently rub the grease spot until it's gone.

- To clean a hamburger grill or pancake griddle, pour brewed coffee onto the surface (the surface can be warm or cold). Wait a few minutes, then wipe clean with a soft cloth—make sure the surface has cooled before you do this.

Dishwasher

- Remove dried-on food or detergent from the chrome inside your dishwasher by rubbing with a piece of lemon. Wipe clean with a damp cloth, then rub dry with a clean, dry cloth.

- Add 1/2 cup vinegar to an empty dishwasher and run the rinse cycle. This will clear any clogs in the dishwasher drain lines and deodorize the machine.

Microwave

- If your microwave is spattered with old sauces and greasy buildup, place a glass measuring cup with 1 cup water and 1/4 cup vinegar inside microwave. Boil for 3 minutes, then remove the measuring cup and wipe inside of oven with a damp sponge.

- Microwaves are veritable safe-deposit boxes for odors. Clean the inside and outside with a little baking soda on a damp sponge; rinse well. Between uses, keep an open box of baking soda in the closed microwave. Change it every 30 days.

- To remove the lingering smell of burned microwave popcorn, heat a small glass dish of pure vinegar in the microwave for 5 minutes on a low heat setting. Remove and wipe down inside of oven.

- Deodorize your microwave by keeping a dish of vinegar inside overnight. If smells persist, change vinegar and repeat procedure nightly.

Coffee & Tea

- Buildup in a coffeemaker's brewing system can affect coffee flavor. Get rid of buildup by running a brewing cycle with cold water and 1/4 cup vinegar. Follow with a cycle of clean water. If you can still smell vinegar, run another cycle using fresh water.

- Remove coffee stains and mineral buildup from the glass pot of an automatic drip coffeemaker by adding 1 cup crushed ice, 1 tablespoon water, and 4 teaspoons salt to the pot when it is at room temperature. Gently swirl mixture, rinse, and wash as usual.

- To clean a teapot or stovetop percolator, fill it with water, add 2 or 3 tablespoons baking soda, and boil for 10 to 15 minutes. After cooling, scrub and rinse thoroughly.

- To clean the inside of a teapot, add the peel of 1 lemon per 2 cups warm water. Soak overnight.

Be Nice to Your Nose

- Garlic and onion odors on countertops respond to a solution of 1 tablespoon bleach and 1 cup water. Wash the surface, then let the solution sit for about 5 minutes. Rinse well.

- If you come home to a foul-smelling fridge full of leftovers you forgot to trash before your trip, toss the mess immediately. Clean up any excess with a sponge or a paper towel, then gather 6 or more coffee filters. Fill each filter with 1/2 cup baking soda; place 1 or more on each shelf and compartment to absorb odors quickly. Remove when odor is gone.

- Kitchen odors disappear thanks to the freshening power of lemons and a few spices. Fill a small pot with water. Add several pieces of lemon rind and about 1 teaspoon each of whole cloves and rosemary leaves. Bring to a boil. The aroma will soon reach nearly every room of your house.

- Freshen the air in your kitchen with the simplest of methods. Heat the oven to 300 degrees Fahrenheit and place a whole lemon on the center rack. With the door slightly ajar, let the lemon "cook" for about 15 minutes; turn off oven. Let lemon cool before removing it.

- Disguise burnt smells with a touch of ground cinnamon. Sprinkle a bit in a pie plate and place in a warm oven for about 10 minutes.

- Boil 1 tablespoon vinegar in 1 cup water to eliminate smoky smells in the kitchen.

- Freshen a plastic lunch box by filling it with water and 1/4 cup vinegar. Let stand for 12 hours, then rinse with fresh water.

- An open box of baking soda in the refrigerator or freezer absorbs odors for up to 3 months.

- To remove odors from a garbage disposal, cut up a lemon, toss it in, and grind it up. Oranges and limes also work to freshen the disposal.

- Remove fish, onion, or garlic odor from hands with a solution of 3 parts baking soda to 1 part water or Ivory Liquid Hand Cleanser. Rub, then rinse.

- Alternately, rub a few coffee beans in your hands; the oil released absorbs the odor. Wash your hands with soap and warm water once the odor is gone.

- To remove onion odor from your hands, sprinkle on a little salt, then moisten with a bit of vinegar. Rub hands together and rinse.

- If your hands smell like garlic, rub a cut lemon over them.

Preventing Mess While You Cook

- Ingredients such as dried fruits won't stick to a knife if you rub a bit of vegetable oil on the blade before chopping.

- Mix and dispense in 2 easy steps—no cleanup required! Mix ingredients for deviled eggs or stuffed mushrooms by placing all ingredients in a plastic food storage bag. Seal it and knead to blend contents. To dispense the mixture, snip off a small corner of the still-sealed bag. Then just squeeze and stuff! When you're done, throw away your "dispenser."

- When you need cracker crumbs for a recipe, put your crackers in a plastic food storage bag and squeeze out most of the air. Seal it almost all the way, leaving it open at the corner so air can escape. Crush crackers by rolling a rolling pin up and down the bag. This contains the mess, crushes the crackers, and keeps your rolling pin clean.

- Before you prepare food on a countertop, cover the surface with a large sheet of either wax or parchment paper. Put it under any cutting boards too. This is especially important when working with meat, chicken, or fish.

- Spread a sheet of aluminum foil on the oven rack below a baking pan if you fear boilovers and spills. (Don't spread the foil on the bottom of an oven.)

- Pots are less likely to boil over when you use this tiny tool: a tiny toothpick laid flat between the lid and the pot. The space allows just enough steam to escape to prevent boilovers. This works when baking covered casserole dishes too.

- Melt chocolate without the messy bowl or pan to wash afterward. Pour chocolate chips, squares, or pieces into a plastic food storage bag and squeeze out most of the air. Seal and place bag in a pan of warm (but not boiling) water. When the chocolate is melted, snip off a small corner of the still-sealed bag; squeeze it into a recipe or use it to decorate a cake.

- Keep that cookbook clean while you cook. Open it to the proper page, then cover it with or enclose it in a plastic food storage bag.

• Picking up the mess from a dropped egg can be tricky. Make it easier by sprinkling the mess with salt and letting stand 15 minutes. The salt absorbs and solidifies the runny egg. Wipe away with a paper towel.

• If you spill a small amount of cooking oil, sprinkle it with salt. Wipe up spill after about 15 minutes.

• Clearing the table after a big dinner party can be a challenge. To get a head start on doing the dishes, line a large bowl with a plastic grocery bag, handles overlapping the edges. Place it prominently in your kitchen with a rubber spatula alongside. As the plates are brought into the kitchen, scrape the scraps right into the bowl. Once the plates are clean, it's a snap to pick the bag up by the handles and toss.

• Save yourself some steps and keep your countertops neater. Line a coffee can with a small plastic bag; place it near the sink and fill it with peelings and scraps. Make just 1 trip to the kitchen trash to toss the bag when you're done rather than traipsing back and forth.

• When you can't wash the breakfast dishes immediately, sprinkle plates with salt to keep eggs from sticking and make dishes easier to clean later.

• Soft cheese or other sticky food stuck on a grater? Cut a lemon in half and rub the pulp side on both surfaces of the grater.

• Place an entire roll or coil of garbage bags in the bottom of your garbage can. When you fill up one bag, remove it and just pull up a new one.

Food Hacks

• To keep hamburger patties separated in the freezer, place a plastic coffee can lid between each one. Store them all in a plastic freezer bag. When the time comes to cook them, the patties will separate easily, even when frozen.

• Cookies lift off a cookie sheet easily if you run a piece of unflavored dental floss underneath them.

- Picking silk from a freshly shucked ear of corn can be a tedious job. Speed up the process by wiping a damp paper towel across the ear; it will pick up the strands.

- Dry lettuce faster than you can say "spin cycle"! Wash the leaves and shake off as much water as you can. Place them in a plastic grocery bag lined with paper towels. Grasp the bag by the handles (or let your kids have the fun) and whirl it around in circles until the lettuce is dry.

- Keep potatoes from sprouting by storing apples with them.

- Hard cheeses that are difficult to cut can be tamed by cutting through them with unflavored dental floss.

Storage & Containers

- Save space and keep place mats handy by hanging them inside a pantry or cabinet door. Clip a set together with a binder clip.

- Group cloth napkin sets together in a drawer or hall pantry with a binder clip. When it's time to set the table for company, you'll have a full set at the ready.

- After the dishes are washed and you're ready to store them, insert a flattened coffee filter between china plates and saucers—or other delicate pieces—to protect them.

- Clean mineral deposits and neutralize any acids in old canning jars by shaking a solution of 4 tablespoons baking soda per quart of warm water inside. Rinse thoroughly, then sterilize as usual.

- Plasticware, especially food containers, often takes on a greasy feeling. Put a capful of bleach in the dishwater along with your usual dishwashing liquid. Problem solved!

- Scrub stained plastic storage containers with a paste of lemon juice and baking soda.

- Avoid red tomato stains on plastic by spraying a container with cooking spray before adding tomato-based food. Before washing the container, rinse with cold water.

Glassware

- Crystal is best washed by hand, very carefully. After washing, dip crystal in a sink full of warm water and 1 tablespoon vinegar. Finish with a clear water rinse.

- Get rid of the cloudy film on glassware by soaking items overnight in a tub of equal parts vinegar and warm water. Wash glasses by hand the next day.

Silver

- Give silverware a quick polish: Sprinkle some baking soda on a damp cloth or a sponge. Rub, rinse, and let dry.

- Shine up your silverware with a banana peel. Remove any leftover "strings" from the inside of the peel, then rub the peel on cutlery and serving pieces. Buff with a clean, soft cloth or a paper towel.

- Make a paste of cornstarch and water and apply to tarnished silverware. Let dry; wipe clean with a dry cloth.

- If you need clean silver now instead of tomorrow morning, pour lemon juice over the piece. Polish with a soft, clean cotton cloth.

- To clean sterling silver pieces and bring back their shine, rub them with a paste made of 1/2 cup distilled white vinegar and 2 tablespoons salt. Dip a clean, soft cloth in the paste, then gently rub silver pieces using a circular motion. Rinse, then dry with another soft cloth.

- To remove silver tarnish, bring a medium-size pot of water to a boil and add 1/2 teaspoon salt and 1 to 2 teaspoons baking soda. Reduce heat. Place tarnished silverware and a piece of aluminum foil in the pot. Simmer for 2 to 3 minutes. Rinse the silverware well, then use a soft cloth to buff dry.

- Place 1 or 2 pieces of white chalk in your silverware chest to prevent tarnishing.

Pots, Pans & Knives

- Burned-on grease in a pot or pan can be removed by filling the pan with water and adding 6 Alka-Seltzer tablets. Let the pan soak for at least an hour, then scrub it clean.

- To loosen baked- or dried-on food in a pan, gently boil water and baking soda in the pan. When food is loosened, allow pan to cool and then wipe clean.

- Don't struggle to scrape off burned-on food in a pan. Pour in a can of Pepsi; allow pan to soak for about an hour, then wipe clean.

- Get rid of excess grease in a roasting pan by sprinkling it with salt and wiping with a damp sponge or paper towel. Wash as usual.

- Reduce the chore of washing a greasy baking dish or pan. After the grease is drained off, rub the pan with a thick slice of lemon or a used lemon half turned inside out. Wash as usual.

- To remove rust from knives, cast-iron pots, and other kitchen equipment, make a paste with 1 part lemon juice and 2 parts salt. Apply with a clean, soft cloth and rub away the rust. Rinse with clear water; dry well.

- Get rid of rust on a kitchen knife by cutting an onion. Using the rusted blade, carefully cut into (but not all the way through) a large, whole onion. Repeat 2 or 3 times. If there is a large amount of rust on the blade, it may require a few more strokes to clean it off.

- To make stains vanish from aluminum or enamel cookware, fill the pot or pan with water and add a cut lime. Boil until the stains are gone. For a small pot, use half a lime; for a larger one, use both halves.

The Smallest Room

Bathroom, restroom, watercloset, loo—whatever you call it, you have to keep it clean. If there's a growing collection of dust balls under your bed or a month's worth of newspapers on your coffee table, you can live with that. But if there is one cleaning job that really must be done each week no matter what, it's cleaning the bathroom.

You can make this unpleasant task a whole lot easier if you and everyone else who uses the bathroom quick-cleans it every day. Most bathrooms are made of materials that are easy to keep clean. Tile and porcelain surfaces are stain-resistant if dirt and scum are not allowed to build up on them. Make it a firm rule in your home to rinse out the tub or shower stall immediately after you use it. Rinse it while you are still wet and in the tub or stall. Simply spray water from the shower head on all interior surfaces, then lather soap onto a damp sponge, swish it around the tub or stall, and rinse. The basin can be given a similar treatment each evening by the last person who uses it.

Keeping tile and porcelain surfaces clean so that they never need to be scoured not only saves time, but it also protects these surfaces from unnecessary wear and keeps them looking their best.

Multi-Surface Cleaners

- Try this basic cleanser for everyday bathroom cleanup. Mix together 3 tablespoons baking soda, 1/2 cup ammonia, and 2 cups warm water. Or skip the ammonia and mix 1 box (16 ounces) baking soda, 4 tablespoons Dawn dishwashing liquid, and 1 cup warm water. Mix well and store in a clearly labeled spray or squeeze container. Be sure to wear rubber gloves and use in a well-ventilated area.

- To keep the bathtub and tiles free of soap scum, rinse thoroughly after each use, and rub the surfaces with a cut lemon. The same method—rubbing surfaces with a cut lemon—can remove many sink and tub rust stains.

- Undiluted bleach in a spray bottle tackles serious bathroom grime. Spray the tub, sink, ceramic tile, or shower surfaces, wait a few minutes, and wipe clean with a damp sponge.

Mildew Busters

- When mildew is multiplying in out-of-the-way spots, place a few cotton balls soaked in bleach in the area. Wait a few hours, then wipe clean with a sponge dampened with warm water.

- Mix equal amounts of vinegar and water in a spray bottle. Spray onto mildewed areas and let sit for 15 minutes. Wipe clean.

- Undiluted isopropyl rubbing alcohol can remove small areas of mildew buildup on grout, caulk, or tile. Dip a cloth into the alcohol and scrub.

- Mildew may make a habit of building up on your shower and tub accessories. Mix 1 1/2 cups bleach with 2 gallons water and scrub bath mats, curtains, and soap dishes with the mixture, using a sponge or a scrub brush. Rinse.

Showers & Bathtubs

- To clean gunky shower tracks, wrap very fine steel wool around an old toothbrush and scrub the tracks. Spray glass cleaner all over the tracks; wipe clean.

- Loosen up soap scum on shower doors and walls by spraying them with vinegar. Let dry, then respray to dampen. Wipe clean. Reapply and let sit for several hours. Then dampen and wipe clean again.

- Shower curtains can become dulled by soap film or plagued with mildew. Keep vinegar in a spray bottle near your shower, and squirt shower curtains once or twice a week. No need to rinse.

- Fight mildew stains and lightly clean a shower curtain by sprinkling baking soda on a sponge and scrubbing. Rinse well.

- To remove mineral and mildew stains from a shower curtain, first soak it in salt water for 15 to 20 minutes. Hang to drain excess water. Rub the stains with lemon juice while the curtain is still damp. Wipe with a damp sponge, rinse with clean water, or run through the washing machine.

- Prevent mildew growth on a shower curtain by soaking it in a bathtub full of salt water (1/2 cup salt to the tub). Soak for several hours, then hang to dry.

- Those sunflower decals may have looked cute when you stuck them on the tub to prevent slips and falls, but now they're chipped, stained, and probably out of fashion. To get rid of them, loosen the glue by saturating each decal with vinegar. (Warm vinegar in microwave for about 3 minutes for better results.) Let vinegar sit for a few minutes, then peel off decals. You should be able to remove any leftover glue by scrubbing with a damp sponge.

- Clear a slow drain by dropping in a couple of Alka-Seltzer tablets. Pour in 1 cup vinegar, then flush with hot water.

- To clear a slow drain, pour in a 2-liter bottle of Pepsi. You'll soon see the drain emptying more quickly.

- For routine cleaning of sink and tub drains, pour in 1/2 cup baking soda followed by 1 cup distilled white vinegar. Let sit for 10 to 20 minutes, then flush with very hot water.

Sinks

- Attack stubborn rust stains in a sink (or tub) with a paste of cream of tartar and hydrogen peroxide. Apply the paste, then scrub clean with a nonabrasive pad or brush. Rinse completely.

- A dryer sheet can control odor and musty smells under your bathroom sink.

- Plug the drain in your bathroom sink, pour in 1/2 cup vinegar, then fill the sink with water. Let sit 1 hour, then scrub any mineral deposit areas with an old toothbrush. Rinse.

- Pour isopropyl rubbing alcohol on a paper towel to remove smudges and hairspray from chrome faucets.

- Clean chrome with club soda. Pour some on a clean, soft cloth and dab it on. Buff to a shine with a second cloth.

Grout

- For tough grout or tile stains, use a paste of 1 part bleach to 3 parts baking soda.

- Grout grime grating on you? Combine the following in a bucket: 2 cups bleach, 3 cups isopropyl rubbing alcohol, 1/2 cup Original Pine-Sol Brand Cleaner, and 1 quart water. Pour the mixture into a plastic spray bottle. Spray and clean away!

- Use a paste of baking soda and water to remove mildew stains on grout. Apply, scrub with an old toothbrush, and rinse.

- For everyday cleaning of tile and grout, rub with a little apple cider vinegar on a sponge. This gives off a pleasant scent and will help cut any greasy buildup.

Deodorizing

- Sprinkle baking soda in the bathroom trash can after each emptying.

- Add a perpetual air freshener to the toilet area by keeping baking soda in a pretty dish on top of the tank. Add your favorite scented bath salts to the mix if desired. Change every 3 months.

- When you hang a new roll of toilet paper, loosely roll up a dryer sheet and place it inside the paper core. The fresh scent will disperse through the small room.

HOUSEHOLD HACKS
FROM ANCIENT HISTORY

- Around 600 B.C., the Phoenicians made soap from goat's tallow (fat) and wood ashes; they sometimes used it as an article of barter with the Gauls.

- The Celts used animal fats and plant ashes and named the product *saipo,* from which the English word soap is derived.

- Beginning in the second century A.D., at the suggestion of the Greek physician Galen, soap was used for washing and cleaning (instead of as a medicine).

Toilets

- Once a week, pour 2 cups vinegar into toilet and let it sit. (Tip: Rest toilet bowl brush inside bowl with lid closed to remind yourself and family members not to use the toilet until it gets brushed!) After 8 hours or more, brush toilet well; flush. This regular treatment will keep hard-water stains at bay and clean and freshen your bowl between major cleanings.

- A half cup of baking soda in the toilet bowl will work for light cleaning. Let sit for 30 minutes, then brush and flush.

- Remove stubborn stains in the toilet bowl by scrubbing with fine steel wool dipped in baking soda.

- To remove toilet bowl stains, pour in a can of Pepsi. Wait 1 hour, then brush bowl clean and flush.

- Clean your toilet by putting 2 denture cleanser tablets in the bowl and letting them sit overnight. Scrub the toilet in the morning.

- Clean your toilet while you're not even home! Pour 1/4 cup bleach into the bowl, but don't flush the toilet until you return—even days later. (Be sure to close the bathroom door before you leave if pets will be around.)

- Wish you could turn those slippery slivers of soap into something other than trash? Collect them in a sandwich-size food storage bag. When the bag is about half full, place it in a pot of warm—but not boiling—water. Remove when the soap melts. When it cools, you'll have a new bar of soap.

- Alternately, whenever a bar becomes too small to handle, cut slits in a sponge and tuck in the soap pieces. Or, put the slivers in a clean child-size sock to make a soaped-up washcloth. Both are perfect for your child's bath time.

- Bring some order to that bathroom or bedroom drawer. A plastic ice cube tray is the perfect organizer for small items such as bobby pins, hair clips, safety pins, earrings, rings, and spare change.

- A large binder clip placed on the end of a tube of toothpaste or similar packaging will ensure that you'll get all your money's worth.

- Soak toothbrushes overnight in a solution of 4 tablespoons baking soda to 1 quart warm water.

- Soak dentures, athletic mouthguards, retainers, or other oral appliances in a solution of 2 teaspoons baking soda dissolved in a glass of warm water. Another option is to scrub these items using an old toothbrush dipped in baking soda.

- So that you won't misplace frequently used items, glue small magnets on the walls of the medicine cabinet to hold nail files, cuticle scissors, clippers, and other small metal objects.

- Your medicine cabinet will stay neat and clean with shelf paper made of blotters that can absorb medicine or cosmetic spills.

Oh, Baby!

Your bundle of joy can unfortunately produce bundles of mess. And when you're the parent of a baby or toddler, you have a lot of demands on your time and energy. These hacks can help.

General Tips

- Sprinkle baking soda on a damp sponge to wipe down cribs, changing tables, baby mattresses, and playpens. Rinse areas thoroughly and allow to dry.

- Remove odors from cloth strollers or car seats by sprinkling baking soda on the fabric. Wait 15 minutes (longer for strong odors) and vacuum.

- Use baking soda directly on metal, plastic, or vinyl strollers, car seats, and high chairs. Scrub using a damp sponge. Rinse and wipe dry.

- Why spend money on an expensive store-bought drop cloth? Split open the seams of one or two trash bags; place on the floor under a high chair.

Bathroom Matters

- Keep diaper pails smelling fresh by sprinkling baking soda over dirty cloth diapers. Line the bottom of a diaper pail with baking soda after you empty it to control odors.

- Accidents happen, especially during potty training. In lieu of a plastic or rubber mattress pad, place several sheets of aluminum foil across the width of a mattress. Cover them with a beach towel or two, then put on a cloth mattress pad and bottom sheet.

- To remove urine from a mattress, first blot dry with a towel or rag. Then sprinkle area with baking soda. Let dry thoroughly, then vacuum.

Toys

- Clean and deodorize vinyl toys with a solution of 1 tablespoon baking soda per cup of water. Wash toys with a damp cloth or sponge, rinse, and dry. For tough stain removal, sprinkle baking soda directly on a damp sponge and scrub. Bring a small spray bottle of this same baking soda solution with you on outings with baby for quick cleanups.

- Disinfect baby toys by cleaning them with a splash of vinegar added to hot water or by soaking them in a dishpan of hot water and 1/2 cup distilled white vinegar.

- Cloth toys can get grungy. To clean without water, sprinkle on baking soda as a dry shampoo; let sit 15 minutes, then brush off.

- Deodorize really smelly stuffed animals by placing them in a paper bag, adding baking soda, and shaking the closed bag vigorously. Store in bag overnight. If necessary, change the baking soda and repeat until the odor is gone.

- Here's another method for cleaning stuffed animals or other cuddlies: Place a toy or a few small ones into a medium to large plastic bag. Add some cornstarch to the bag, close tightly, and shake. Brush the toys clean.

Clothing

- If your baby spits up on his shirt or yours, moisten a cloth, dip it in baking soda, and dab at the spot. The odor will be controlled until the clothing can be changed.

- For tough stains on baby clothes, soak the items (colorfast only) in a bucket of water with 1/4 cup bleach added. Wait 10 minutes, rinse in clean water, then launder as usual.

There's Something Smelly in the State of Your House...

Despite your best efforts to keep things clean, sometimes you still walk down into the basement, open a closet, or return from vacation and think that you smell something musty in your house. Here are some tips to help.

Throughout the House

- Combine 1 teaspoon baking soda, 1 tablespoon vinegar, and 2 cups water. Stir; mixture will foam up a bit but this will soon subside. Store the solution in a clearly labeled spray bottle. Spray a mist in the air anywhere you want to eliminate or control household odors.

- Pour vinegar into shallow bowls and set them out to absorb odors in areas of your home where odors are a problem. Make sure the bowls are out of reach of small children and pets.

- To make a homemade air freshener, fill a coffee filter with baking soda and close it with a twist tie. Place it where the air is less than fresh—in the refrigerator, closet, your car, shoes, boots, or anywhere.

Garbage Cans

- Periodically wash out and deodorize garbage cans with a solution of 1 cup baking soda per gallon of water.

- Reduce garbage can smells by sprinkling baking soda inside each time you add garbage.

- Before you replace the trash bag in a stinky garbage can or diaper pail, pour some nonclumping cat litter in the bottom. When the litter gets damp, change it.

- When you put out your trash in plastic bags, coat the outside of the bags with a little ammonia. The smell should keep strays away. Consider spraying the outside of your trash cans with ammonia too.

Paper

- To clean musty items such as old postcards, magazines, sheet music, and books, place the items in a paper bag with some baking powder. Seal bag and change powder every few days until odor disappears.

- You can refresh musty old magazines found in cellars or garages if the pages aren't stuck together. Just lay the magazines out in the sun for a day. Then sprinkle baking soda on the pages and let sit for an hour or so. Brush off.

- Dry out the moisture in a damp book by sprinkling the pages with cornstarch and letting it sit overnight. Brush out the cornstarch in the morning. This even works on mildewed books. Cover the mildew spots with cornstarch and let sit for a few days. Brush off the powder outdoors, so the mildew spores won't find a new home in your home.

- Cat litter will freshen up musty-smelling items, such as books or old magazines. Put the items in a paper bag; carefully pour in about 1 cup litter. Check on the progress and replace the litter every other day till the job's done.

- Reduce the dampness and prevent mildew in a closet or basement with white chalk. Tie together 12 sticks with a string or put several sticks in a knee high pantyhose. Hang the chalk in the damp area; replace every few months.

- A closet with bare wood floors can begin to smell stale. To freshen the whole closet, lightly mop the floor with a mixture of 1 cup baking soda and 1/2 cup vinegar in 1 gallon warm water.

- Deodorize a closet by placing a shallow box of cat litter on the floor— even if you don't have a cat. Keep the door shut. In a few days, the air should be fresher.

- Turn your closet into a cedar closet. Fill a large plastic food storage almost to the top with cedar chips (available at pet stores). Seal the bag and poke small holes all over both sides. Hang it in your closet.

- Make a sachet for dresser drawers: Pour potpourri into the toe portion of pantyhose or knee highs. Tie a knot right above the potpourri and cut off the remainder of the hosiery.

- The enticing aroma of herbal tea suits a sachet perfectly. Choose your favorite flavor or scent, open a tea bag or two, and pour the leaves into pantyhose or knee highs. Tie a knot right above the tea and cut off the remainder of the hosiery.

- Fill the toes of an old pair of pantyhose with baking soda, cut off the legs, and tie to secure. Hang the sachets anywhere musty odors linger.

- To keep dressers, sideboards, and linen closets smelling nice, grab a few new, unwrapped bars of bar soap. Wrap each in facial tissue and place them in drawers and on shelves.

- Fill a snack- or sandwich-size food storage bag with potpourri. Seal it and poke several small holes to make an effective yet inexpensive sachet for your dresser drawers.

- Eliminate mildew odors in drawers and on various other surfaces by wiping the affected area with full-strength antiseptic mouthwash. Wipe clean with a paper towel.

- If your cedar chest or closet no longer smells of cedar, lightly sand its surfaces. Sanding opens the wood's pores and releases a fresh cedar scent. Remember that the scent doesn't kill moths; it merely repels them. So it's best to clean clothes before storing to remove any moth eggs.

Bags, Trunks, Hampers & More

- To combat the aroma inside an odor-collector such as a laundry hamper, shoe, or diaper pail, place a dryer sheet inside it.

- Deodorize a canvas bag or any bag that has developed a musty smell by sprinkling the inside with salt, zipping up the bag, and letting it sit overnight. Shake out the salt in the morning and allow bag to air out.

- An old trunk can smell mighty musty. To get rid of the odor, haul the trunk outside for some sunlight and fresh air. Pour a light layer of baking powder in the bottom and close the lid. Every few days, sweep out the old and sprinkle on some new powder. Repeat until the smell is gone.

- If that old trunk smells stale and musty when you open it, empty it out and give it a little fresh air. Let it sit outside in the sunshine, open wide, for several hours. When you bring the trunk inside, sprinkle a layer of cat litter on the bottom and close the lid. Replace the litter every other day until the odor is gone.

- Control odors in shoes that are starting to smell by sprinkling the insides with a little salt. Let sit overnight, then shake out the salt. The salt will help control moisture, which contributes to odors.

- Tuck dryer sheets under your chair or couch cushions to help freshen furniture.

- You can also pack a dryer sheet in your suitcase or gym bag. It will protect your clean clothes from the odors of your dirty ones.

- Control odor from a pet accident by leaving a thin layer of baking soda on the affected area after cleaning. Vacuum when dry.

While on Vacation

- If your bathroom never seems to be fully dry and you are going away for some time, place a large, shallow box of nonclumping cat litter in your bathtub to absorb moisture.

- If you're going away for the weekend, deodorize your fridge while you're gone. Just pour some clean cat litter onto a cookie sheet and place it on the middle shelf of the fridge. Discard upon your return.

- If you own a summer cabin or other building that will be shut up for a long period of time, prevent damp, musty odors from taking over while you're gone by filling shallow boxes with cat litter and storing one in each room of the house.

Don't Let the Walls Close In

Walls and ceilings get dirty in the same passive way: Grime and dust float through the air, land on them, and stick. But walls also get dirty in more active ways—when toddlers try out their crayons, chocolate-bar eaters switch on lights, and exuberant chefs toss spaghetti. Unless you deal with the passive dirt buildup on walls, attempts to wipe up after your active family will result in a smeary mess or leave a streak of clean-wall color in sharp contrast to the rest of your wall.

Wallpaper

- Take a grease spot off wallpaper by first blotting it with a paper towel and then applying cornstarch to the area. Gently rub off the corn starch, then vacuum the area using an upholstery brush attachment.

- General soil comes off when a piece of rye bread is wadded up and used like an eraser.

- Baking powder gently but thoroughly removes dirt and grime from delicate wallpaper. Make a paste with water and baking powder and apply it to your wall with a sponge. Wipe clean with another damp sponge.

- Mix 1/2 cup vinegar and 1 quart water and apply solution to dirty wallpaper using a sponge. Be careful not to saturate, especially at seams and corners, or you could loosen wallpaper.

Wood/Wood-Paneled Walls

- Mayonnaise will get rid of white water marks on wood paneling. Rub a small amount into each mark; let soak in overnight, then wipe clean.

- Bring out the shine of varnished woodwork with cold Lipton tea. Wipe it onto the wood using a soft cloth; rinse with cool water and a sponge. Dry with a clean cloth.

Painted Walls

- Mix 1/2 cup vinegar, 1 cup clear ammonia, 1/4 cup baking soda, and 1 gallon warm water. Caution: Wear rubber gloves, and work in a well-ventilated area when using this powerful solution. Apply the solution to the wall with a sponge and rinse with clear water.

- If your walls have a rough texture, use old nylon stockings or socks rather than a sponge because they won't tear and leave difficult-to-remove bits on the surface.

Brick Walls

- A wall made of brick requires little attention if you use your vacuum cleaner to remove loose dirt regularly. A solution of hot water and an all-purpose cleaner will clean accumulated dirt and stains from the surface.

- If the brick wall is especially dirty, use a commercial brick cleaner and a stiff-bristled brush. Rinse with clear, hot water, and wipe dry.

Removing Crayon Marks

- If your young artist has chosen crayon as a medium and a painted wall as a canvas, use a baby wipe to gently erase the marks.

- Remove crayon marks from walls with a damp sponge dipped in baking soda.

- Erase crayon marks and drawings from painted walls by rubbing them with Crest toothpaste on a soft cloth. Rinse away with warm water.

- Cornstarch can remove crayon marks from wallpaper. Mix a little with water to make a thick paste, then dab it on the affected area. Let dry completely, then brush off.

Rooms with a View

You can avoid washing your windows by keeping the drapes drawn, the shades down, or the blinds closed. But life without windows is a little gloomy, so we suggest that you plan to wash your windows twice a year, usually in the spring and in the fall. If you get everyone in the household involved in window washing, you can probably finish the task on a Saturday morning. Put some of your crew to work inside and others outside. Tell those who are at work in the house to use vertical strokes; those working on the outside should use horizontal strokes. With this method, you can quickly track down streaks.

Wash windows from the top down to prevent drips on sections you've already cleaned. Use a soft toothbrush or cotton swab to clean corners.

Soap will leave smudges on windowpanes, and abrasive cleansers or steel wool will scratch the glass. Window cleaners themselves pose a threat to woodwork. If the cleaner is allowed to drip on the windowsill, it can harm the paint or varnish.

If you wash windows on a hot or sunny day, the glass is more likely to streak.

Windows

- Wash windows with a sponge dipped in baking soda. To avoid dry haze on the windows, rinse them with a clean sponge and plenty of water before drying.

- Clean your windows with club soda. Pour some on a clean cotton cloth; wipe windows. Using a second cloth, dry them right away.

- To spot-clean a window or other glass surface, use isopropyl rubbing alcohol.

- The simplest and easiest method of making window cleaner is to add 2 tablespoons vinegar to 1 cup water. Spray solution on windows, and wipe with paper towels.

- Make your own streak-free window cleaner: Thoroughly mix 2 tablespoons cornstarch, 1/2 cup ammonia, and 1/2 cup vinegar in a bucket of 3 to 4 quarts warm water. Pour the milky solution into a spray bottle. Spray on windows; wipe with warm water. Rub dry with a paper towel or lint-free cloth.

- Here's another window-cleaning solution: Fill a clean, empty spray bottle with 1/2 cup vinegar, 1/4 cup isopropyl rubbing alcohol, and enough water to fill. Spray on windows or glass, and wipe with paper towels.

- Wash greasy kitchen windows with a solution of 2 tablespoons lemon juice, 1/2 cup distilled white vinegar, and 1 quart warm water.

- Washing a window with intricate panes? Dip a Q-tips cottonswab into your cleaning solution and negotiate all those corners.

Blinds, Shades & Screens

- Put dirty venetian blinds in a tub of warm water; add 1/2 cup baking soda, soak for half an hour, then scrub and rinse.

- To prevent dust and pet hair from sticking to window blinds, turn the blinds to the closed position, spray with Static Guard, and let dry.

- Window shades that can't be washed using liquid will come clean if you rub them with a terry cloth towel dipped in a little bit of yellow corn meal.

- Dip a damp wire brush into baking soda and use it to clean door and window screens. Scrub, then rinse screens with a sponge or a hose.

Carpets and Rugs

For spilled popcorn, wayward crumbs, and crunched potato chips, a handheld vacuum will swoosh away the mess in seconds. But eventually you'll have to clean the entire floor. You can rely on an upright vacuum cleaner to clean carpets and rugs quickly and thoroughly.

The easiest way to tackle a large job, like vacuuming a wall-to-wall-carpeted room, is to break it down into sections. When you mow the lawn, you make sure you go over all of it. When you vacuum wall-to-wall carpeting, you can be sure to cover every inch if you divide the floor into quarters. Vacuum an entire quarter before moving on to the next.

It's a good idea to vacuum your rugs and carpets about once a week, or more often in areas of heavy traffic. We're not just talking about hallways and the route to the kitchen. People move their feet around when they sit and grind dirt from their shoes into the carpeting, so you'll need to pay special attention to the carpet in front of chairs and couches, and under desks. Vacuum areas of heavy traffic with a crisscross pattern of overlapping strokes. Every so often take a little extra time and use your crevice tool for in-depth cleaning around baseboards and radiators and in other hard-to-reach places.

Prevention

- To prevent your family from tracking dirt all over your house, keep a box of baby wipes near the door and have each person clean his or her shoes before entering. (Removing shoes at the door is another excellent practice.)

- A surefire way to cut your cleaning time in half is to put thick mats or throw rugs at all the entrances to your home, both inside and outside the doors. These mats intercept and trap loose dirt, keeping it from being tracked through your house. Compared with cleaning a whole room, throwing a washable rug into the washing machine or vacuuming a doormat takes practically no time at all.

General Cleaning

- For general cleanup of problem areas on carpets or rugs, use equal parts vinegar and water. Lightly sponge solution into carpet, rinse, and blot dry. Let dry completely.

- To make a carpet and upholstery shampoo, use an eggbeater to mix 1 quart water, 1/4 cup Tide laundry detergent, and 1 tablespoon vinegar. Whip until a stiff foam forms. Gently rub into fabric or carpeting, then remove soiled foam by scraping with a dull knife. Follow with a rinse of clean water.

- A basic cleanser for nongreasy stains: Combine 1/4 teaspoon Dawn dishwashing liquid with 1 cup lukewarm water and blot onto a stain until it's gone. Rinse well and blot with paper towels until dry.

- Try removing grease spots from a rug with a mixture of 1 part salt and 4 parts isopropyl rubbing alcohol. Rub vigorously in the same direction as the nap, then rinse with water. For a larger rug, wipe off the solution with a damp cloth and blot dry. (Protect wood floors by placing several layers of paper towels underneath the rug beforehand.)

Revive and Freshen Your Carpets

- This treatment will help keep your carpet fresh and clean longer between shampoos: Combine 1/4 cup vinegar and 1 gallon water, then use solution in a steam-cleaning vacuum after shampooing your carpet to remove any residue.

- Once a month, sprinkle carpets with baking soda. Let sit overnight, then vacuum.

- Revive your carpets by sprinkling cornstarch all over them. Wait 30 minutes, then vacuum and admire the clean.

- Mix 1 cup crushed, dried herbs (rosemary, southernwood, lavender, etc.), 1 teaspoon ground cloves, 1 teaspoon ground cinnamon, and 1 teaspoon baking soda. Combine ingredients, and sprinkle over carpet. Let sit for a few minutes, then vacuum.

- Mix 1 small box baking soda with a few drops of your favorite essential oil; sprinkle mixture onto carpet. Let sit 10 to 20 minutes, then vacuum.

- Use 1 cup baking soda, 1 cup cornstarch, and 15 drops essential oil fragrance. Leave on carpet 10 to 20 minutes, then vacuum. Store mixture in a glass jar or airtight container.

GREAT MOMENTS IN
CLEANING HISTORY

1869 Ives McGaffey patents a wood-and-canvas "sweeping machine"—the country's first hand-pumped vacuum cleaner—and calls it the Whirlwind.

1901 British engineer Hubert Cecil Booth invents the "vacuum cleaning pump," a large, horse-drawn wagon containing a gas-powered pump and long hoses.

1908 Department-store janitor James Spangler staples a broom handle to a soapbox, then attaches an old fan motor and a pillowcase; he improves the model and patents the first commercially successful portable electric vacuum cleaner, which comes with a cloth filter bag and attachments.

1922 William Hoover, husband of Spangler's cousin, invests in and becomes president of the sweeper company. He renames it for himself: the Hoover Company

Special Problems

- If the spot remover you use alters the color of your carpet, try touching up small places with artists' acrylic paint. If that doesn't work, try a felt-tip marker or a permanent-ink marker of the appropriate color. Go slowly and blend the color into the fibers.

- To raise depressions left in carpet by heavy furniture, try steaming. Hold a steam iron close enough for steam to reach the carpet, but don't let the iron touch the fibers, especially if they are synthetic, because they could melt. Lift the fibers by scraping them with the edge of a coin or spoon.

- If a carpet thread is loose, snip it level with the pile. If you try to pull out the thread, you risk unraveling part of the carpet.

- To repair a small area burned down to the carpet backing, snip off the charred fibers, and put white glue in the opening. Then snip fibers from a scrap of carpet or an inconspicuous part of the carpet (perhaps in a closet). When the glue gets tacky, poke the fibers into place. If the burn isn't all the way down to the backing, just snip off the charred tips of the fibers with scissors. The slightly shorter length of a few carpet fibers will never be noticed.

- To repair a large burned area in a carpet, cut out the damaged area and substitute a patch of identical size and shape. Secure the new piece of carpeting with double-faced carpet tape or a latex adhesive.

Carpet Stain-Removal Guide

The first rule of carpet cleaning is to wipe up any spill or stain immediately. Often undiluted vinegar can be your best bet for removing a new stain.

This quick-reference guide points to the best cures for the most common carpet spots and stains.

Acid Stains

- Acid spills, such as toilet-bowl cleaner, drain cleaner, and vinegar, demand especially quick action. Dilute them immediately with baking soda and water or with club soda. You can tell by feel and smell when the acid spill has been cleaned up. Then apply a solution of ammonia (1 part) and water (10 parts). Rinse with cold water, let dry, and vacuum.

Alcoholic Beverages

- If someone spills an alcoholic drink on your carpet, quickly dilute the spot with cold water so that the alcohol does not have time to attack the dyes. Absorb the excess liquid. Then mix 1 teaspoon mild detergent, 1 teaspoon white vinegar, and 1 quart warm water. Apply the solution to the spot. Let the carpet dry. If the spot remains, reapply the solution. Let the carpet dry completely. Vacuum gently.

Blood

- Absorb as much of the blood as you can. Then mix 1 teaspoon mild detergent, 1 teaspoon white vinegar, and 1 quart warm water. Apply the solution to the spot. Let the carpet dry. Apply dry-cleaning fluid, and let the carpet dry completely. Vacuum gently.

Butter

- The first step in cleaning up a butter spill is to scrape up as much solid butter as you can or to absorb all the melted butter that you can. Apply dry-cleaning fluid. Let the carpet dry. If the spot remains, reapply the fluid, and let the carpet dry thoroughly. Then vacuum.

- You can also sprinkle some cornstarch on a butter stain or other greasy spot on your carpet. Let dry completely, then vacuum.

Candle Wax

- The easiest way to remove candle wax from your carpet is to press an ice cube against the drip. The wax will harden and can then be pulled off. Treat any remaining traces of wax with dry-cleaning fluid. Let the carpet dry, and vacuum.

- Another way to remove candle wax on carpeting is to place a blotter, brown paper bag, or a thick layer of paper towels over the spilled wax, and press with a warm iron until the blotter absorbs the melted wax. Move the blotter frequently so that it doesn't get oversaturated. Remove traces of the wax with spot remover. Let dry, and then vacuum.

Candy

- Candy that contains no chocolate is usually easily removed from carpet. Scrape up as much of the candy as you can. Mix 1 teaspoon mild detergent, 1 teaspoon white vinegar, and 1 quart warm water. Apply the solution to the spot. Let the carpet dry. If the spot remains, reapply the solution. Let the carpet dry. Vacuum gently.

Chewing Gum

- Chewing gum can be a sticky mess, so harden it by pressing an ice cube against the blob of gum. The gum will harden and can then be pulled off. Treat any remaining traces of the chewing gum with dry-cleaning fluid. Let the carpet dry, and then vacuum.

- When chewing gum is stuck in a carpet or rug, put a few ice cubes in a plastic food storage bag and place it directly on the gum. When gum hardens, use a dull knife to scrape it off.

- To dissolve chewing gum stuck in carpet or on any cloth, saturate area with vinegar and let it sit briefly. (For faster results, heat vinegar first.) Carefully tug at gum to remove it.

Chocolate

- The longer chocolate is allowed to stay on your carpet, the more difficult it is to remove. Scrape the chocolate from the carpet. Mix 1 teaspoon mild detergent, 1 teaspoon white vinegar, and 1 quart warm water. Apply the solution to the spot. Rinse well with clear water, making sure you don't drench the carpet. Let the carpet dry. Vacuum gently.

- Clean chocolate stains from carpeting with a mixture of 1 part vinegar and 2 parts water. Sponge on mixture, and blot stain with clean cloths until gone.

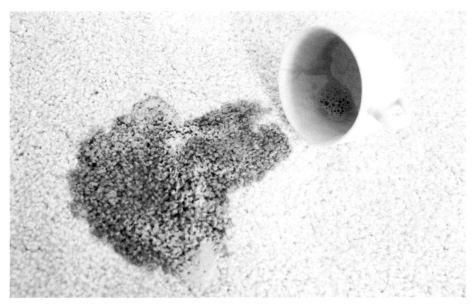

Coffee

- Blot spilled coffee immediately. Then mix 1 teaspoon mild detergent, 1 teaspoon white vinegar, and 1 quart warm water. Apply the solution to the spot. Let the carpet dry. Apply dry-cleaning fluid, and let the carpet dry again. Vacuum gently.

- Clean coffee stains from carpeting with a mixture of 1 part vinegar and 2 parts water. Sponge on mixture, and blot stain with clean cloths until gone.

- To remove a coffee or tea stain from a rug or carpet, pour a small amount of beer directly on the spot. Gently rub in the beer with a cloth or a sponge; blot with a paper towel. Repeat until the stain is gone.

- Blot up a fresh coffee spill on your carpet with baby wipes—they are absorbent and nongreasy, so they won't add to the stain.

Crayon

- Dropped crayons have a knack for getting stepped on and ground into carpeting. Scrape away excess crayon and remove the rest by placing a blotter over the crayon stain and pressing it with a warm iron until the blotter absorbs the melted crayon. Move the blotter frequently so that it doesn't get oversaturated. Apply dry-cleaning fluid, and let the carpet dry. Reapply if necessary, and then vacuum.

- Remove crayon stains from carpeting or any other fabric or surface by scrubbing area with a toothbrush dipped in vinegar.

Egg

- Like all protein stains, spilled eggs need to be cleaned up immediately. Scrape up as much cooked egg as possible or mop up raw egg. Mix 1 teaspoon mild detergent, 1 teaspoon white vinegar, and 1 quart warm water. Apply the solution to the spot. Let the carpet dry. If the spot remains, reapply the solution. Let the carpet dry. Vacuum gently.

Fruit

- Fruit stains can be very hard to remove if they are allowed to set, but if you act quickly this method usually prevents a permanent stain. Scrape up spilled fruit, and absorb fruit juice. Mix 1 teaspoon mild detergent, 1 teaspoon white vinegar, and 1 quart warm water. Apply the solution to the spot. Let the carpet dry. If the spot remains, reapply the solution. Let the carpet dry. Vacuum gently.

Glue

- A spot of dried white school glue can be taken out of a carpet with a mixture of 1 part vinegar and 2 parts water. Just sponge on and blot. If the spot is stubborn, cover it with warm vinegar and let it sit for 10 to 15 minutes. When glue has softened, either scrape it up using a dull knife or blot with paper towels.

Gravy

- If you accidentally rock the gravy boat, wipe up as much of the spilled gravy as you can. Mix 1 teaspoon mild detergent, 1 teaspoon white vinegar, and 1 quart warm water. Apply the solution to the spot. Let the carpet dry. Apply dry-cleaning fluid. Let the carpet dry. Vacuum gently.

- To get rid of a gravy stain on your carpet, first remove as much liquid as possible by covering the spot with salt. This will prevent the greasy stain from spreading. Then follow rug manufacturer's instructions to clean. For this and other stubborn stains, you may need a dry-cleaning solution or an enzyme detergent.

Hand Cream

- When you inadvertently squirt hand lotion on your carpet, wipe up the spill immediately. Apply dry-cleaning fluid. Let the carpet dry. If the spot remains, reapply the dry-cleaning fluid. Let the carpet dry, and then vacuum.

Ink

- Fast action is essential when you spill ink on carpet. Immediately apply dry-cleaning fluid. Let the carpet dry. If the spot remains, reapply the dry-cleaning fluid. Let the carpet dry thoroughly, and vacuum.

- Remove ink stains from carpet with cornstarch. Start with about 2 tablespoons cornstarch, then slowly add enough milk to make a paste. Apply paste, wait a few hours, and brush it off.

Ketchup

- Clean ketchup stains from carpeting with a mixture of 1 part vinegar and 2 parts water. Sponge on mixture, and blot stain with clean cloths until gone.

Lipstick

- Open tubes of lipstick have a way of falling into the hands of curious toddlers or just falling, period. When your carpet acquires a telltale trace of lipstick, scrape away as much of the lipstick as you can. Apply dry-cleaning fluid, and let it dry; then mix 1 teaspoon mild detergent, 1 teaspoon white vinegar, and 1 quart warm water. Apply the solution to the spot. Let the carpet dry. If the spot remains, reapply the solution. Let the carpet dry. Vacuum gently.

Mildew

- The first step in removing mildew stains is to kill the fungus. To do this, mix 1 teaspoon disinfectant cleaner and 1 cup water. Apply the solution to the mildewed carpet, and blot. Then to remove the stain, apply a solution of ammonia (1 part) and water (10 parts). Blot, rinse, and let dry. Vacuum. Keeping the area totally dry is the only way to prevent the reoccurrence of mildew, which can eventually break down carpet fibers.

Milk

- Blot up the spilled milk. Mix 1 teaspoon mild detergent, 1 teaspoon white vinegar, and 1 quart warm water. Apply the solution to the spot. Let the carpet dry. Vacuum gently.

Mud

- When muddy boots and shoes get past the mats at the entrances to your home, allow the mud tracked onto your carpeting to dry completely, and then brush or scrape off as much as possible. Mix 1 teaspoon mild detergent, 1 teaspoon white vinegar, and 1 quart warm water. Apply the solution to the spot. Let the carpet dry. If the stain remains, apply dry-cleaning fluid and blot dry. When the spot is completely dry, vacuum gently.

Oil

- Blot up an oil spill on a rug or carpet right away, then sprinkle baking powder directly on the spot. Let dry, then vacuum up the residue...and the stain!

Nail Polish

- Apply dry-cleaning fluid or amyl acetate, acetone, or nail-polish remover to the spilled polish. Test the solvent you plan to use on an inconspicuous part of the carpet. Never apply acetate, acetone, or nail-polish remover to acetate carpet fibers. If the stain remains, mix 1 teaspoon mild detergent, 1 teaspoon white vinegar, and 1 quart warm water. Apply the solution to the spot. Let the carpet dry. Vacuum gently.

Salad Dressing

- A misplaced slosh of salad dressing can be removed easily from most carpeting. Absorb as much salad dressing as you can. Mix 1 teaspoon mild detergent, 1 teaspoon white vinegar, and 1 quart warm water. Apply the solution to the spot. Let the carpet dry. If the spot remains, reapply the solution. Let the carpet dry. Vacuum gently.

Salt Deposits

- Mix equal amounts of vinegar and water, and use a sponge to apply solution to salt deposits on your rug or carpet. Do not saturate. Let dry, then vacuum.

Soft Drinks

- The carbonation in soft drinks will help you clean spilled drinks quickly, but act fast because some of the dyes in the drinks can permanently stain your carpet. Blot up the spilled drink. Mix 1 teaspoon mild detergent, 1 teaspoon white vinegar, and 1 quart warm water. Apply the solution to the spot. Let the carpet dry. If the spot remains, reapply the solution. Let the carpet dry. Vacuum gently.

- Clean cola stains from carpeting with a mixture of 1 part vinegar and 2 parts water. Sponge on mixture, and blot stain with clean cloths until gone.

Tar

- Remove tar or other stubborn sticky stuff from carpet fibers by rubbing vegetable oil into the substance. Rub the substance loose, then blot with a paper towel.

Tea

- The tannic acid in black tea is a potent dye, so move quickly when tea is spilled on your rug. Blot up the tea spill. Mix 1 teaspoon mild detergent, 1 teaspoon white vinegar, and 1 quart warm water. Apply the solution to the spot. Let the carpet dry. Apply dry-cleaning fluid. Let the carpet dry. Vacuum gently.

- To remove a coffee or tea stain from a rug or carpet, pour a small amount of beer directly on the spot. Gently rub in the beer with a cloth or a sponge; blot with a paper towel. Repeat until the stain is gone.

Urine

- Mix 1 teaspoon mild detergent, 1 teaspoon white vinegar, and 1 quart warm water. Apply the solution to the spot. Let the carpet dry. If the spot remains, reapply the solution. Let the carpet dry. Vacuum gently.

- Don't panic when a toddler or your pet has an accident on your carpeting. As soon as you can, blot up as much urine as possible with paper towels, then pour on the club soda. Let sit 1 to 2 minutes and blot again. Repeat if necessary. To remove any last traces, mix equal parts distilled white vinegar and cool water; scrub the solution into the affected area using a stiff brush. Blot up the liquid and rinse with cool water.

Vomit

- Treat vomit quickly. Blot up as much as possible, then dilute immediately with baking soda and water or with club soda. Then apply a solution of ammonia (1 part) and water (10 parts). Rinse with cold water, let dry, and then vacuum.

Wine

- When red wine is spilled on your carpet, dilute it with white wine, then clean the spot with cold water, and cover with table salt. Wait ten minutes, then vacuum up the salt.

- Immediately blot up all moisture from a red wine spill, then sprinkle the area with salt. Let sit 15 minutes. The salt should absorb any remaining wine in the carpet (turning pink as a result). Clean entire area with a mixture of 1 part white vinegar and 2 parts water.

Carpet Free = Carefree?

There are probably many different kinds of hard-surface floors in your home. Your vacuum cleaner can help you maintain all the floors in your home, from the concrete in your basement to the parquet under the rug in the living room. Weekly vacuuming is not all it takes to keep a hard-surface floor looking its best. So here are a few quick and easy cleaning methods to help you speed through the heel marks and the sticky stuff that accumulate on your hard-surface floors, as well as some strategies for minor floor fixes.

General

- To prevent scratching the floor when moving heavy furniture across uncarpeted areas, slip scraps of carpeting, pile down, under the furniture legs.

Wood Floors

- If your wood floors are clean but a bit dull, mop cooled Lipton tea over them. Let them air-dry, then buff to a shine with a clean towel.

- To polish a varnished wood floor, put a folded bath towel into one leg of a pair of pantyhose and start buffing!

- Remove water spots on wood floors with a sponge dampened in a solution of 4 tablespoons baking soda and 1 quart warm water.

- To remove chewing gum stuck to a hardwood floor, set a food storage of ice cubes atop the gum. After gum hardens, use an old credit card to pry it loose. If necessary, polish that area of the floor after gum is removed.

- Add 1 cup vinegar to 1 gallon of water; mop lightly onto hardwood floors (do not saturate). No need to rinse. This will keep floors shiny and remove any greasy buildup.

- If you have a squeaky wood floor under tile or carpet, you may be able to eliminate the squeak without removing the floor covering. Try to reset loose boards by pounding a hammer on a block of scrap wood in the area over the squeaky boards. The pressure may force loose nails back into place.

- You may be able to silence a squeaky wood floor by using talcum powder as a dry lubricant. Sprinkle powder over the offending areas, and sweep it back and forth until it filters down between the cracks.

- Try filling dents in a wood floor with clear nail polish or shellac. Because the floor's color will show through, the dents will not be apparent.

Tile

- Clean tile floors with 1/2 cup baking soda in a bucket of warm water. Mop and rinse clean.

- Make ceramic tile floors shine by mopping with a mixture of 1 cup vinegar and 1 gallon warm water.

- Add extra shine to your clean, dry tile floor. Wrap a piece of wax paper around a dust mop and sweep it over the floor.

- Wash grout between terra-cotta tiles with straight vinegar to clean up and prevent smudges.

- WD-40 can remove the following (and likely many more things) from tile floors: scuff marks, mascara, gum, coffee stains, crayon, ink, marker, adhesives, rubber cement, and glue.

- To remove a floor tile for replacement, lay a piece of aluminum foil on it and then press down with your iron set at medium. The heat of the iron will soften the tile's adhesive, and you can easily pry up the tile with a putty knife or scraper.

- To remove a damaged floor tile, soften it with a propane torch fitted with a flame-spreader nozzle. (Be careful not to damage surrounding tiles.) When the tile is soft, pry it up with a putty knife and scrape the old adhesive off the subfloor so that the replacement tile will bond cleanly.

- You can remove a floor tile by covering it with dry ice. Wear work gloves to protect your hands. Let the dry ice stand for ten minutes. The cold will make the tile brittle, so it will shatter easily. Chisel out the tile from the edges to the center.

- Laying floor tile will be easier if the room temperature is at least 70 degrees Fahrenheit before you start, because tile is more pliable at higher temperatures. Put all boxes of tile in the room for at least 24 hours prior to positioning tiles on the floor. Try to keep the room temperature at the same level for about a week after laying the tiles, and then wait at least a week before washing the floor.

- After laying floor tiles, you can help them lie flat by going over them with a rolling pin.

Linoleum

- Scrub a linoleum floor with a mixture of 1 gallon water and 1 cup vinegar. If floor needs a polish after this, use straight club soda.

- Mop up salt deposits from winter boots with a mixture of equal parts vinegar and water.

- Mix 1/2 cup vinegar, 2 tablespoons furniture polish, and 1 gallon cool or cold water. Mop the floor with this mixture, using a sponge or string mop.

- Sometimes you can flatten bulges or curled seams in a linoleum floor by placing aluminum foil over them and ironing them with your iron. (The heat will soften and reactivate the adhesive.) Position weights, such as stacks of books, over treated areas to keep them flat until the adhesive cools and hardens.

Asphalt

- Mix 1/4 cup low-sudsing, all-purpose cleaner; 1 cup ammonia; and 1/2 gallon cool or cold water. Caution: Wear rubber gloves, and work in a well-ventilated area when using this powerful solution. Apply the cleaner to the floor with a sponge mop, using pressure for heavily soiled areas. Rinse with cool, clear water for spotless results. Apply two thin coats of a water-based, self-polishing floor finish, allowing the floor to dry between coats.

- Mix 1/2 cup vinegar, 2 tablespoons furniture polish, and 1 gallon warm water. Caution: Wear rubber gloves. Mop the floor with this mixture, using a sponge mop or string mop.

Concrete

- Mix 1/4 cup low-sudsing, all-purpose cleaner; 1 cup clear ammonia; and 1/2 gallon cool or cold water. Caution: Wear rubber gloves, and work in a well-ventilated area when using this powerful solution. Apply to the concrete floor with a sponge mop, using pressure for heavily soiled areas; rinse with cool, clear water for spotless results. Let the floor dry.

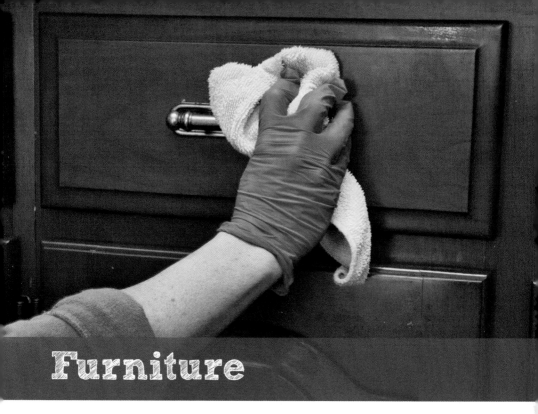

Furniture

If your home is like most, much of your furniture probably does all kinds of things it wasn't intended to do. The upholstered chair by the front door is a catchall for schoolbooks and jackets. The dining table doubles as a sewing table, desk, or computer center. And many of us practically live in bed, snacking, reading, watching TV, or just recovering from the day at work. Grime builds up on the chair, lint sticks to the dining table, and cracker crumbs work their way into the mattress. Fortunately, we've found that you can maintain (or restore) the good looks of most furniture with the proper care.

Wood Furniture

- To remove dirt, grime, and built-up polish from wood furniture, brew some tea. Steep 2 Lipton Tea Bags in 4 cups boiling water; let cool. Dampen a soft, clean cloth with tea and wipe down the dirty surfaces. Polish with a soft, clean cloth.

- Beer: It's not just for stacking in pyramids on the coffee table. Clean wood furniture, especially oak and mahogany, with warm beer. (It's okay if it's stale.) Using a clean, soft cloth, wipe it on the wood; wipe dry with a second cloth.

- To remove a surface mark from a wood table, whether a water mark or a scald from a hot dish, make a thin paste of vegetable oil and a pinch of salt. (Use about 1/8 to 1/4 teaspoon salt per tablespoon of oil.) Just wipe on paste with a soft cloth, then buff lightly as you wipe it off.

- Apply mayonnaise to white rings, spots, or crayon marks on your wood furniture, let it sit for 1 hour, then wipe clean with a soft cloth or sponge.

- Remove paper that's stuck on a wood surface by generously applying cooking spray. Wait 5 to 10 minutes, then carefully remove the paper.

- Dusting carved wood furniture can be difficult. Use a Q-tips cotton swab for the small spaces. Additionally, a swab dipped in furniture polish is a great tool for shining and protecting your beautiful furniture.

- Try this recipe for homemade furniture polish. Whisk 1/2 teaspoon extra virgin olive oil and 1/4 cup white vinegar in a small bowl. Pour mixture into a clean, resealable jar and label clearly. When ready to use, give jar a good shake, then apply polish liberally to wood surfaces with a soft cloth. Wipe away excess.

- Here's another homemade polish for general use on all wood furniture. In a glass jar with a tight-fitting lid, mix 1/4 cup fresh or store-bought lemon juice with 1/2 cup vegetable oil. Apply to wood furniture with a cotton cloth, rubbing in a small amount at a time. Kept out of direct sunlight, this mixture can be stored for several months.

- To remove scratches from a wood table, increase the amount of lemon juice in the previous furniture polish recipe so that you're using equal parts lemon juice and vegetable oil. With a soft, clean cotton cloth, gently rub the mixture into the wood, buffing out the scratches. Repeat as needed until scratches are gone.

- Remove waxy buildup on wood tabletops with a solution of equal parts water and vinegar. Wipe onto area, then rub and dry immediately using a soft cloth.

- To restore luster to mahogany furniture, mix 3 tablespoons vinegar and 1 quart water. Dip a sponge in the mixture, wring thoroughly, then use to wipe wood. Do not saturate.

- After polishing any wood furniture in your home, sprinkle a bit of cornstarch over the surface. Then use a clean, soft cloth to buff it to a high shine. Any excess oil will be absorbed by the cornstarch.

- If the old wood boards you acquired have great potential (and a great amount of grime), try this cleanser. Mix 3 parts sand, 2 parts Ivory Liquid Hand Cleanser, and 1 part lime juice thoroughly in a bucket. Using a stiff brush, scrub the wood with the cleanser. Rinse with water; rub dry with a clean towel. Now get on with making that furniture!

- Look for levelers, mechanical devices built into the furniture's base that compensate for uneven floors, when you buy tall pieces of furniture such as china cabinets and wall units.

Upholstered Furniture

- Upholstered furniture should not be placed in constant, direct sunlight or near heating outlets; this can cause fading or discoloration.

- To remove spilled grease from upholstery, cover the spot right away with cornstarch. Wait until as much of the grease as possible has been absorbed, then vacuum. Repeat if necessary.

- To remove an oily stain from upholstered furniture, grind about a cup of cat litter into a powder and scatter it over the stain. Wait until the oil is absorbed, then vacuum up the litter.

- A fresh grease stain on a cloth chair can be absorbed with equal parts baking soda and salt. Sprinkle the mixture onto the stain and rub lightly; leave on for a few hours, then vacuum.

- A trick for removing lint and pet hair from upholstery is to rub the fabric with a dryer sheet.

- Pick up pet hair easily by wrapping your hand with a piece of duct tape with the sticky side out. Run your hand along the upholstery and pick up the hair.

Leather

- Keep a leather armchair looking like new. Every few weeks, wipe it with a soft cotton cloth that's been dipped in beaten egg white. Buff to a shine with a second cloth.

- To keep leather upholstery looking its best, give it a milk bath. Every 3 months, use a clean cloth to wipe on a small quantity of skim milk.

Vinyl

- Clean vinyl upholstery, such as that on a recliner or kitchen chair, with a paste of baking soda and water. Rub on, allow to dry, then wipe off.

- Clean up spots on vinyl furniture by wiping with a cloth dipped in undiluted vinegar.

- Erase ink stains from vinyl surfaces by rubbing on a bit of vegetable shortening with a cloth or paper towel. Use a little elbow grease and scrub until stains disappear. Wipe clean with a fresh towel.

Glass

- To bring out the shine in a glass tabletop, rub it gently with a few drops of lemon juice. Dry with a paper towel, then polish with a piece of crumpled-up newspaper.

Wicker & Cane

- Prevent white wicker furniture from yellowing by scrubbing it with a stiff brush moistened with salt water. Let dry in full sunlight.

- Clean cane furniture with baking powder. Wet the cane with warm water, then apply the powder with a paintbrush. Let dry; brush off. Rinse with cold water and allow to air-dry.

Fans

- After cleaning the blades of a fan (any kind: freestanding, oscillating, or ceiling fan), wipe the surfaces with a dryer sheet. This will slow the accumulation of hair, dust, and dirt.

Treasures, Decorative Items, and Oddball Knicknacks

Your prize possession may be a collection of pewter salt-and-pepper shakers depicting national monuments or the box of bone-handled knives your brother gave you on your birthday. The decorative objects you've collected and cherish add visual interest to your home and sometimes become treasured family heirlooms. They'll also need to be cleaned from time to time. Most of your things can be safely cared for at home, especially if frequent dusting has kept dirt from building up on their surfaces.

Pianos

- Restore yellowed piano keys to their original shine with mayonnaise or vinegar. Rub on a small amount with a soft, dry cloth; wipe clean with a damp cloth. Do not saturate. Polish to a shine with another dry cloth.

- Bring back the shine on piano keys and gilt picture frames by rubbing carefully with a cloth dipped in milk.

- To clean and remove stickers from the keys of pianos and synthesizers, all it takes is a little WD-40 and a clean cloth.

Mirrors

- Make your mirrors shine by washing them with a bucket of water combined with 1 tablespoon ammonia.

- Your mirror will sparkle after this tea break. Brew a pot of strong Lipton tea; let cool. Dip a soft cloth into the tea, then wipe it over the whole mirror. Buff with a soft, dry cloth.

Metals: Silver, Brass, Copper & Pewter

- To remove silver tarnish using a process called ion exchange, boil a pot of water and 1/2 teaspoon salt with 1 to 2 teaspoons baking soda. Place the tarnished pieces of silverware in a pan with the saltwater solution along with a piece of aluminum foil. Soak for 2 to 3 minutes. Rinse the silverware well, then use a soft cloth to buff dry.

- Clean and polish your precious metals with chalk. Sprinkle a little powdered chalk onto a clean, damp cloth. Rub a tarnished piece until shiny. Rinse with water; dry.

- To remove salt stains from a silver saltshaker or another silver piece, rub with extra virgin olive oil. Let sit a few days, then wipe with a clean cotton cloth.

- Because pewter is a soft metal that can be damaged easily, it must be cleaned gently. Add enough all-purpose flour to a mixture of 1 teaspoon salt and 1 cup distilled white vinegar to make a smooth paste. Apply paste to a pewter piece with a soft cloth. Let dry (about half an hour); rinse with warm water. Polish with a soft cloth, making sure to remove paste residue from grooves and hidden areas.

- To clean a pewter piece, immerse it in water that has been used to boil eggs. Wait a few minutes, then gently rub the pewter with a soft cloth dipped in the same water. When the item is clean, rinse it with clear water and wipe dry.

- Ammonia is perfect for pewter polishing. Mix 2 tablespoons ammonia with 1 quart hot, soapy water. Wipe the surface of the pewter piece using a soft cotton cloth.

- To clean and shine copper or brass surfaces, combine equal parts salt and all-purpose flour and add enough distilled white vinegar to make a paste. Rub the paste on with a soft cloth. Let sit about 1 hour, then wipe off and buff with a clean, soft cloth.

- Use either of these pastes to clean brass or copper. For the first, mix lemon juice with either baking soda or cream of tartar to form a paste. The second combines lemon juice, salt, and corn meal. Rub the paste onto the brass or copper using a soft cloth; rinse and dry.

- Clean slightly tarnished brass or copper by rubbing with half a lemon or lime dipped in salt.

- Remove stubborn tarnish from copper by spraying stains with distilled white vinegar and sprinkling with salt. Scrub with a sponge, then rinse thoroughly, making sure to remove all traces of salt. Repeat if necessary.

- To remove "greenery" from brass and copper, rub the surface with a solution of equal parts ammonia and salt. Rinse with clear water.

- Remove marks on bronze by wiping bronze items with a soft cloth dampened with turpentine.

Lacquer

- To polish lacquered metal items, rub the surface with a soft cloth dampened with a few drops of extra virgin olive oil.

- The stronger, the better: Apply strongly brewed Lipton tea with a soft cloth to wash and polish black lacquer figurines and other decorative pieces. Use a second cloth to wipe dry.

Vases

- To clean a glass vase or similar container, fill it three-quarters full with hot water, add a teaspoon of baking soda, and shake. Let soak, then rinse.

- Remove mineral deposits or stains from a vase by dampening surfaces with water and sprinkling with salt. Wipe with a clean cloth.

- Clean stains from a vase by dropping 2 Alka-Seltzer tablets in the vase with water. Let sit, swish liquid around, and rinse.

- Get rid of stubborn spots on porcelain lamps, vases, and candlesticks by dipping a damp cloth in baking soda and rubbing them away. Wipe clean with a damp cloth.

Candles

- Wipe dirt from candles with a soft cloth, a folded paper towel, or a cotton ball dipped in isopropyl rubbing alcohol.

- You can forget about digging old, melted wax out of candlesticks. Before you insert a candle, coat the inside of the holder with petroleum jelly or baby oil.

- To release candle stubs and dripped wax that are stuck in or on candlesticks and holders, try soaking them in warm water or blasting them with a blow-dryer. A far neater and more effective method is putting the candlestick or holder in the freezer for at least 24 hours. The stub or wax drippings will slide away easily!

- Candle wax can be removed from most hard surfaces with a paste of baking soda and water. Scrub with a nylon scrubber.

Marble

- To clean marble, wipe with a damp, soft cloth that's been dipped into powdered chalk. Rinse with clear water, using another cloth or a sponge. Dry completely.

Organization and Storage

You can never find your keys. Or you put something away in a drawer, and when you need it again, you find it's gotten tangled or even broken. Here are some hacks to prevent those things from happening.

Everyday Items

- Hang a basket near the front door and keep your keys in it. You'll always know where they are. Also use this basket for bills and letters that need to be mailed. When you grab your keys, you'll remember to pick up the mail as well.

- Hang a wicker basket on the bathroom wall for storing towels, tissues, soap, or bath toys.

- Install two rows of coat hooks on your closet doors— one down low for a child to use, another higher up for you to use.

- A metal garbage can is perfect for storing long-handled yard tools. Hooks can also be attached to the outside of the can for hanging up smaller tools. You can lift up the whole can and move it to whichever part of the yard you're working in.

- Use an extra slot in the toothbrush holder to keep a medicine spoon handy.

- Keep toothbrushes handy but neatly out of the way on cup hooks attached to a wall or under a cabinet.

- Keep your wet umbrella in the shower where it can drip without making a mess. This is an especially useful strategy when you have company on a rainy day and everyone has an umbrella.

- A good place to store small clothing items is in large, metal potato-chip cans—after the cans are washed.

- Put a wine rack next to the door and use it to store your sandy beach shoes and muddy running or gardening shoes.

Lights & Batteries

- Keep flashlight batteries fresh by storing them in a sealed plastic bag in the refrigerator.

- To minimize breakages, store loose light bulbs in tumblers. A paper towel wrapped around the bulb before you put it in the tumbler provides added protection.

Linens

- Most people don't use good cloth tablecloths and napkins every night or even every week. To prevent the creases that form when linens are folded for storage, roll the linens onto cardboard tubes covered with cling wrap. Use paper towel tubes for napkins and gift wrap tubes for tablecloths.

- Incidentally, fine table linens are much easier to iron if you first place them in a plastic food storage bag and refrigerate them for 6 to 24 hours. Remove them from the bag before ironing!

- Keep place mats flat and out of the way by hanging them on a clipboard hung from a hook inside a cabinet or pantry door.

Cords

- To keep an appliance cord neat, store it in an old paper towel tube (use half a tube for short cords). Gather up the cord in loops a few inches longer than the tube; slide tube over looped cord. Label the tube with the name of the corresponding appliance.

Books

- Keep old books from becoming musty in storage. Before stowing them away, put a dryer sheet between the pages in a few places.

Luggage

- Before storing a piece of luggage, place an open box of baking soda inside and close the luggage overnight. Repeat this when removing luggage from long-term storage.

- Send mildew odor packing: Toss a bar of scented bath soap into each piece of luggage before storing.

Breakables

Breakables—from glass figurines to porcelain vases—need extra attention before you store them. Carefully place a breakable item in a plastic food storage bag that is just big enough to hold it. Seal the bag until it's almost closed. Blow up the bag with air, then run the seal the rest of the way. When you put the bag in a storage box or container, the item will be protected in a cushion of air.

Blankets

Freshen blankets that have been in storage by sprinkling with baking soda and rolling them up for a couple of hours. Shake out -baking soda, then fluff in the dryer without heat.

Paper Products

Smart shoppers take advantage of good deals. But where do you put all those rolls of toilet tissue and paper towels? Hang a pair of pantyhose on a nail or hook. Slide the rolls, one at a time, down each leg. Cut a hole at the bottom for dispensing; close it up with a twist tie or tie a loose knot until you need a roll.

Cleaning Tools

Cleaning tools with long handles or hoses—such as vacuum cleaner accessories, dryer vent cleaners, and ceiling fan dusters—are cumbersome to store. An old pair of pantyhose can "handle" the job. Hang a pair on a nail or hook, then slide the tools into the legs. If a tool has an extra-long handle, cut a very small hole in a toe of the pantyhose and insert it through the hole. The rest of the tool will stay in the leg.

Nails & Screws

Glass baby-food jars are ideal for storing nails and screws. Better yet, nail the caps to a wood base or wall plaque, and just screw the jars into place.

Creating More Storage Space

- If your home is built with studs and drywall, you can add cabinets between the studs, anywhere you need them—they won't take up any space at all. For example, put a liquor cabinet over your bar, or fashion a canned-goods pantry in your kitchen.

- Pegboard is most often used on walls, but it can also be used as a room divider or to make the inside of a closet or cabinet door more functional. When installing pegboard, remember to provide space behind the panels for the hooks.

- Use flat, roll-out bins for under-the-bed storage. They can hold bed linens, sewing supplies, and infrequently used items.

- To increase the capacity and efficiency of a drawer, outfit it with a lift-out tray. Fill the tray with items you frequently use, and use the space beneath the tray for articles you seldom need.

- Add more storage space in your bedroom by building a headboard storage unit. You can place books, lamps, or a radio on the lid of the unit and inside you can store extra linens and blankets.

- For extra closet storage, see if your closets can accommodate a second shelf above the existing one. If you install the main clothes-hanging rod high enough, you may be able to install another rod beneath it on which to hang shorter items such as slacks and shirts.

- A hallway can double as a storage area. Line it with shelves or shallow cabinets, or put shelving across the width of the hallway.

- If you're in need of an extra closet for storing items like golf clubs, skis, and camping equipment, angle a decorative folding screen across a little-used corner.

- Hooks, shelves, or hanging bins can transform the insides of closet doors into useful storage areas.

- Convert an ordinary closet or chest into a cedar closet or chest by installing thin cedar slats over inside surfaces. Then weather-strip to contain the scent.

- Use a stairway as a storage area by replacing ordinary nailed-in-place steps with hinged steps. The space under the hinged steps can hold boots or sports equipment.

- Put the space under a stairway to work as a storage area. Construct a wheeled, wedge-shaped container that fits into the area beneath the steps.

- To give yourself more storage space in a small bathroom, put up shelves on the dead wall space beside the vanity, over the toilet, or behind the door. Such shelves offer convenient storage without intruding on floor space.

- To make shelves without hammering a nail, upend two narrow wastebaskets on your closet shelf and position another shelf across them. Or use sturdy boxes stacked on their sides to make compartmented shelf space—you can see at a glance what's stored in the boxes, and you can use the tops for little-used items.

Easing Separation Anxiety

When you were a kid, you might have loved placing stickers on everything. As an adult, you worry more about what you'll do when they need to come off. No fear—we've got you covered.

- Remove adhesives, tape, glue, rubber cement, and labels from virtually all surfaces—even paint—with WD-40.

- Not only that, but with the help of WD-40, chewing gum can be removed from all manner of things, including hair, dryer lint screens, bed linens, linoleum floors, and aluminum siding.

- Use a bit of all-vegetable shortening to remove a label, price tag, or adhesive residue from glass, metal, and most kinds of plastic. Just cover the area with shortening. After 10 minutes, carefully scrub it clean with a no-scratch sponge.

- Remove an old sticker from a window, mirror, or other glass surface: Apply some mayonnaise to the area, wait a few minutes, and ease off the sticker with a flexible putty knife. Scrape gently if needed to remove stubborn adhesive.

- Safely scrape a decal, price tag, tape, or stuck-on paper from a wood surface by saturating the surface of the item to be removed with vegetable oil or dampening with vinegar. Let sit 10 minutes, then peel or gently scrape the sticker off. If it still won't budge, set your hair dryer on low and aim it at the item for half a minute. The heat will loosen the glue.

Painting the Town Red—or Just Your Home

Painting a cabinet, a chair, or even a room is an easy way to freshen your home's design. These painting hacks will help.

Preparing to Paint

- To avoid having to clean a paint tray, press a sheet of aluminum foil into it before use. When you're finished painting, simply wrap up the foil and dispose of it. You can also line the tray with a plastic bag, and then discard it when the job's done.

- Make a paint holder from a coat hanger to keep your hands free when painting. Open the hanger and bend it in half; then bend it into an "S" to hook over the ladder and hold your paint can.

- Before using a new paintbrush to apply oil-based paint, soak it for a day in a can of linseed oil. The brush will last longer and be easier to clean.

- Protect doorknobs when painting a door by wrapping the knobs with aluminum foil or by slipping plastic sandwich bags over them.

- Glue paper plates to the bottoms of paint cans to serve as drip catchers. The plates move along with the cans and are more convenient than newspapers.

- If you want to paint a window frame and have no masking tape, use strips of dampened newspaper. They will stick to the glass. Peel off the paper when you finish each frame.

- If your light-switch plate was painted over along with the wall and you now need to remove it, avoid flaking or chipping any paint by cutting carefully around the switch plate with a single-edge razor blade. Remove the screws and lift off the plate.

- If you don't want to—or can't—remove hardware when painting adjacent areas, coat the hardware with petroleum jelly before painting. You'll be able to wipe off any paint that accidentally gets on the metal.

While You Paint

- When painting a ceiling with a roller, it's not necessary to try to keep the roller strokes all the same length. The lines won't show when the paint dries.

- If you're interrupted in the middle of a painting job, wrap aluminum foil or plastic wrap around your brushes and rollers. The wrapping should be loose enough to avoid mashing the bristles on brushes or the pile on rollers but tight enough to keep the air out. Leave the wrapped brushes on a flat surface or hang them up. Put the packet in the freezer to save the brush for a longer period of time.

- Prevent drips when painting a drawer front by removing the drawer and painting it face up.

- To avoid smearing while painting cabinets, paint the insides of the cabinets first. Then paint the tops, bottoms, and sides of doors before painting the door fronts. If you proceed in this sequence, you won't have to reach over already-painted areas.

- When painting stairs, paint alternate steps so that you'll have a way out. When those steps dry, paint the others. Or paint one side of each step at a time. Use the other side for foot traffic until the painted side dries, then reverse the process.

- Don't wipe your paintbrush against the lip of the paint can. The lip will soon fill up with paint that will run down the side and drip off. Use a coffee can to hold the paint instead.

- To cut the smell when you're decorating with oil-based paint, stir a spoonful of vanilla extract into each can of paint.

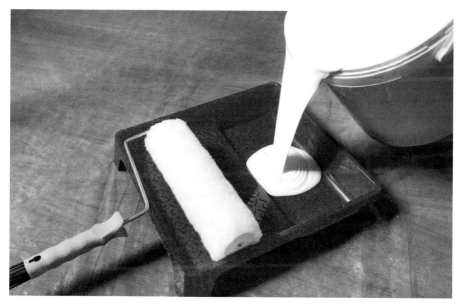

- If you want to be able to use a previous coat of exterior paint as a base for a new coat, the old paint should be no more than five years old. If you wait longer than that you'll have a major job of scraping, sanding, and spackling.

- Wrinkling occurs when too much paint is applied or when the paint is too thick. You can correct wrinkling easily by sanding the surface and brushing on paint of a thinner consistency.

- Artificial light darkens color, so paint will look lighter in the daylight. If you're in doubt about a color at the paint store, take the container outside to examine the color.

- Color can saturate your eyes. When mixing paint, look away at a white surface for several minutes to allow your eyes to adjust so that you can judge the color accurately.

- To get the correct feel for spray painting and to determine the correct spray distance from the object to be painted, first experiment with a sheet of cardboard as the target area.

- Record how much paint is required to cover each room by writing the amount on the back of the light-switch plate. When you remove the switch plate before repainting, you'll be reminded of how much paint you need.

- To avoid painting a window shut, gently slide the sash up and down as the paint hardens but before it forms a seal.

- If you are working on a ladder in front of a closed door, lock the door so that no one can inadvertently swing the door open and send you sprawling.

- When tiny spots need a paint touch-up, use a cotton swab instead of a brush. You won't waste paint, and you won't have to clean a brush.

Cleanup & Storage

- If the smell of fresh paint bothers you, you can eliminate it from a room in one day with a dish of ammonia, vinegar, or onion slices in water left out in the room.

- If you use masking tape around windows while painting the woodwork, remove the masking tape immediately after painting. Otherwise, it may pull off some of the paint.

- To get paint drips off hard-surface flooring, wrap a cloth around a putty knife and gently scrape up the paint. Then wash the areas with warm, soapy water. Don't use solvent; it can damage the finish on the floor.

- Why buy new paint thinner when you can reuse the old? Here's how: Pour paint thinner into an empty coffee can. After you've cleaned your brushes, cover the can tightly and let it stand for several days. When paint from the brushes has settled to the bottom as sediment, drain off the clean thinner into another can and store for reuse.

- To clean a paintbrush without making a mess of your hands, pour solvent into a strong, clear plastic bag, and insert the brush. Your hands will stay clean as you work the solvent into the bristles through the plastic.

- To clean a paint roller after use, roll it as dry as possible, first on the newly painted surface and then on several sheets of newspaper. Then slide the roller from its support and clean it with water or a solvent, depending on the type of paint used.

- Before capping leftover paint for storage, mark the label at the level of the remaining paint so you'll know without opening the can how much is left inside. Label the can with the room the paint was used for, so there's no question which paint to reorder or use for touch-ups.

- If you store a partially used can of paint upside down, skin won't form on the surface of the paint. (Be sure the lid is tight.)

- Leftover paint that is lumpy or contains shreds of paint skin can be strained through window screening.

- To keep a brush as soft as new, clean it and then rinse it in a solution of fabric softener and water.

- An empty coffee can with a plastic lid makes a perfect container for soaking brushes. Just make two slits in the center of the plastic lid to form an "X," push the brush handle up through the "X," and replace the lid. The lid seals the can so the solvent can't evaporate, and the brush is suspended without the bristles resting on the bottom.

- White paint won't yellow if you stir in a drop of black paint.

- You can remove paint spatters from your hair by rubbing the spots with baby oil.

- If you are cleaning brushes or rollers that have been used in oil-based paint, varnish, shellac, or lacquer, work in a well-ventilated area away from open flames.

- Before cleaning a brush, rid it of excess paint by tapping it against the inside rim of the can and then vigorously stroking the brush back and forth on a thick pad of folded newspapers until very little paint comes off.

- Clean brushes and rollers used for shellac in denatured alcohol, then wash in a detergent solution.

- Clean brushes or rollers used for lacquer in lacquer thinner or acetone and then wash in a detergent solution.

- Clean brushes or rollers used for oil-based paints and varnishes in turpentine or paint thinner and then wash in a detergent solution.

- Clean brushes and rollers used for latex paints in water and then wash in a detergent solution. Do not allow brushes to soak in water; this can loosen the bristles.

- Rinse all brushes well after washing and shake vigorously to remove excess water. Comb the bristles with a wire brush to straighten them. Then allow the brush to dry completely before storing it flat or hanging from a rack.

Deck the Halls— and Walls

Your pictures, prints, and decorations help turn your house into a home. These design and decoration strategies will help.

Pictures

- If a picture won't hang straight, wrap masking tape around the wire on both sides of the hook so that the wire can't slip. Or install parallel nails or hooks a short distance apart; two hooks are better than one for keeping pictures in their places.

- Squares of double-faced tape affixed to the two lower-back corners of the frame will keep a picture from moving. If you don't have double-faced tape, make two loops with masking tape, sticky side out. Apply to each of the lower-back corners and press the picture against the wall.

- Take the guesswork out of arranging several pictures on a wall. Spread a large sheet of wrapping paper or several taped-together sheets of newspaper on the floor and experiment with frame positions. When you decide on a pleasing grouping, outline the frames on the paper, tape the paper to the wall, and drive hooks through the paper into the wall. Then remove the paper and hang the pictures.

- Picture hanging can be frustrating if you simply try to eyeball the right spot to put the hook. Instead, place a picture exactly where you want it the first time with the following method: Cut a sheet of paper to the exact size of the frame. Position the pattern on the back of the picture, pull up taut the wire the picture will hang from, and mark the inverted "V" point on the pattern. Adjust the pattern on the wall, and then poke through it to mark the "V" point on the wall. If you nail the hook there, the picture will hang precisely where you wanted it.

- If the picture isn't too heavy, another timesaving method is to hold the picture itself by its wire and decide where you want it positioned. Wet a fingertip and press it on the wall to mark the wire's inverted "V" point. The fingerprint mark will stay wet long enough for you to drive a nail or hook on target.

- Don't lose a perfect picture grouping when you repaint a room—insert toothpicks in the hook holes and paint right over them; when the paint dries, remove the toothpicks and rehang your pictures.

- To prevent a plaster wall from crumbling when driving in a nail or hook, first form an "X" over the nail spot with two strips of masking tape or transparent tape.

- If you're hanging a picture from a molding but don't like the look of exposed picture wire, substitute nylon fishing line. The transparent nylon does a disappearing act that allows your picture to star on its own.

- Hang heavy objects by driving nails directly into the wood studs behind walls. There are several ways to locate studs. You can tap a wall gently with your knuckles or a hammer. A wall sounds hollow between studs, solid on top of them. Or move an electric razor (turned on) along a wall; a razor registers a different tone over studs. If nails were used to attach drywall to studs, a magnet will indicate the location of the nails and, therefore, the studs.

- Sometimes a picture that has been hanging for a while will leave a dark outline on the wall because dust and dirt have collected against the frame. To prevent this buildup, allow better air circulation by holding pictures slightly away from the wall with thumbtacks pressed firmly into the backs of their frames. You can get the same result by fixing small tabs of self-sticking foam weather stripping to the picture backing.

Mirrors

- When hanging a mirror with screws that go through mounting holes in the glass, don't tighten the screws all the way. Leave enough play to prevent the mirror from cracking if the wall shifts.

- Hang mirrors to reflect you but not the sun; some mirror backings are adversely affected by direct sunlight.

Design

- A room will appear larger if you paint an oversized piece of furniture the same color as the walls.

- A small room can be made to look larger if you install mirrors on one wall to reflect the rest of the room.

- The texture of your furnishings can brighten or darken a room. Glossy surfaces like satin, glass, and tile reflect light and add brightness to a room; surfaces like brick, carpet, and burlap absorb light and make a room seem less bright.

- In a room with a low ceiling, use vertical lines—high-backed chairs, straight draperies—to carry the eye upward and give an illusion of height. Horizontal lines—a long sofa or low bookcases—give a feeling of space and make high ceilings appear lower.

- Small rooms will seem even smaller if filled with elaborate patterns or designs. Keep the furniture for a small room simple and the colors fairly restrained.

- A darker color on the ceiling will make a room with a high ceiling seem more in proportion. So will low-placed, eye-catching objects such as a low coffee table, low-slung chairs, and plants on the floor.

- In a long, narrow room, paint the end walls contrasting colors for a striking effect. Room dividers or furniture positioned in the middle of the room will give the effect of two rooms in one and lessen the feeling of length.

- A favorite painting can be the inspiration for the color scheme of a room. Select one dominant color and several contrasting shades to create a pleasing combination.

- If you use the same fabric on two different chairs, it will tie the decor of the room together.

- To add color to matchstick blinds, weave rows of colored ribbon through them.

- Matchstick blinds can disguise a wall of hobby or utility shelves for a clean, unified look. They also can be used to partition off a closet or dressing area.

- There is no need to invest in drapes if your budget is tight. Instead, brighten up inexpensive shades by decorating them with tape to complement the wall color or wallpaper, or by gluing fabric over them.

- To give a room a soft glow, spotlight objects in a room instead of lighting the whole room. For example, light a piece of art or a bookcase.

- Hang shiny, metallic blinds vertically or horizontally to help reflect summer sun. This works especially well in south and west windows.

- You can make a curtain panel from a bed sheet by knotting the top corners around a bamboo pole.

- A screen of hanging plants can be a great substitute for curtains.

- For an insulating window covering, attach wood rings to a patchwork quilt and hang it from a wood rod. Don't do this, however, if the quilt is an antique that could fade or otherwise be damaged by exposure to sunlight.

- Turn your bathroom into a miniature gallery with pictures that can't be damaged by humidity.

- Keep your decorative baskets looking healthy by placing them away from dry heat and rinsing them periodically with clear water to remove dust and restore moisture.

- Display flowers in unusual vases—a crystal ice bucket, a fluted champagne glass, a bright coffee mug, or a jug. Flowers, in fact, look good in almost any container.

- For a quick, easy, and inexpensive way to re-cover a chair, drape a twin-size sheet over the chair, and tie or pin the corners to fit. You can use the same trick to add interest to a small table.

- An easy way to give a room a new look is to update hardware, such as doorknobs, drawer pulls, and curtain rods.

- Replace the drab cord or chain on a light fixture with a piece of satin piping or silver cord. Thread a bright ceramic bead at the end of the cord for a finishing touch.

- Glue pieces of felt to the rough bottoms of vases and art objects to keep them from scratching tables.

- Use leftover dining room wallpaper to make matching place mats. Paste the paper onto sturdy cardboard, trim the edges neatly, and coat each mat with a plastic spray.

- An old dining table found at a flea market can become a sofa-height coffee table. Just cut the legs to the height you need.

- You can make unusual centerpieces in no time by floating flowers in clear glass dishes. Fill the dishes halfway with water, cut the stems from the flowers, and place them in the dishes.

- Old, carved doorknobs, attached to each end of a dowel, make an attractive curtain rod. Paint or stain the knobs to match your furniture.

- You can make cheap floor rugs by stenciling canvas with nontoxic acrylic paints.

- Make an extra closet into a book nook for quiet reading. Remove the door, and install a wall lamp, shelves, and a comfortable chair.

- You can make inexpensive bookcases out of flue tiles or conduit pipes. The cubbyholes are perfect for storing wine.

Your Home Shop

If you own your own home, you likely have a corner of the garage or basement filled with tools of all sorts. It can be a jumbled mess, or it can be a tidy resource. Here's how to make it more the latter than the former.

- To protect tools, store them where they aren't subjected to moisture. Keep a thin coating of oil on metal parts, wrap them in plastic wrap, or keep carpenter's chalk, which absorbs moisture, in the toolbox.

- To sharpen scissors, snip pieces of sandpaper.

- A piece of garden hose, slit open, is a handy protective cover for the teeth of a handsaw between projects.

- Clean tools without expensive cleaners: Pour a small amount of kerosene onto the metal parts of a tool and rub vigorously with a soap-filled steel-wool pad. Then wad a piece of aluminum foil into a ball and rub on the surface. Wipe away the residue with newspaper, and coat the tool lightly with olive oil before storing. **Caution:** Kerosene is flammable; do not use it near an open flame.

- If you hang tools on pegboard walls, outline the tools with paint so you'll know at a glance where each tool goes. You'll also know when a tool hasn't been replaced.

- If you want to remind yourself to unplug an electric drill when changing accessories, fasten the chuck key near the plug end of the cord.

- Paint all tool handles with an unusual bright color, or wrap reflective tape around them; they'll be easy to identify if borrowed or left in the wrong place.

- Don't take a chance of hitting a thumb or finger when hammering a small brad, tack, or nail. Slip the fastener between the teeth of a pocket comb; the comb holds the nail while you hold the comb. A bobby pin or a paper clip can be used the same way as a comb.

- Here's a homemade rust-preventive coating for tools, outdoor furniture, and other metal objects: Combine 1/4 cup lanolin and 1 cup petroleum jelly in a double boiler over low heat. Stir until the mixture melts and blends completely, then remove from heat and pour into a clean jar, letting the mixture cool partially. Use the mixture while it's still warm. Don't wipe it off—just let it dry on the object. If you have leftover coating, cover it tightly, and rewarm it before you use it again.

- An empty soft-drink carton makes a convenient kit for holding and carrying lubricants.

- To keep the pores of your hands dirt- or grease-free, wipe on a thin coat of petroleum jelly before starting a messy task.

- You won't waste time when picking up spilled nails, screws, or tacks if you collect them with a magnet covered with a paper towel. When the spilled items snap toward the magnet, gather the towel corners over the pieces and then pull the towel bag away from the magnet.

- As an aid in measuring lumber or pipe, paint lines a foot apart on your shop or garage floor.

- You can prevent a knot in nylon rope from working loose by holding it briefly over a small flame. The heat will melt and bond the fibers.

- Know the exact width of your hand so you can make rough measurements without using a ruler or tape measure.

- Loosen a stubborn screw, bolt, or nut with a shot of penetrating oil. If you don't have oil, use hydrogen peroxide, white vinegar, kerosene, or household ammonia. Should these prove ineffective, heat the metal with an iron, rap it sharply with a hammer while it's still hot, and try again to loosen it. **Caution:** Kerosene is flammable; do not use it near an open flame.

- You can often loosen rusted bolts by pouring a carbonated beverage on them.

- If a bolt repeatedly loosens due to vibrations, coat the threads with fingernail polish and reinsert it. When you need to remove it, you can break the seal with a little effort.

- If you don't have a carpenter's level, you can substitute a straight-sided jar with a lid. Fill the jar three-quarters full of water. Lay it on its side on the surface you're testing – when the water is level, the surface is, too.

- For easy workshop measuring, fasten a yardstick to the edge of your workbench. Cut keyhole slots in the yardstick so you can remove it when you need it elsewhere.

- If you're out of penetrating oil, you can substitute hydrogen peroxide or lemon juice.

- An old nylon stocking makes an effective strainer if you're out of cheesecloth.

- You can use a coping saw blade to remove a broken-off key from a lock. Slide the blade in beside the key, turn it toward the key so its teeth sink into the key's soft brass, and then pull the blade out along with the key fragment.

- To prevent metal tubing from denting when sawing it, insert a dowel that fits the tube's interior tightly.

- Dipping the ends of a rope in shellac, varnish, or paint will keep them from unraveling.

- To hide a screw head, drill a counter-bored hole, seat the screw, glue a dowel into the counter-bore and sand it flush.

Sleep Tight

Bedspreads, blankets, mattresses, quilts—all require care and attention.
These tips will help you keep them in good shape for a long time.

Bedspreads

- Many bedspreads are washable. Before you wash your bedspread,
  dip a corner of it in the detergent solution you plan to use to check for
  colorfastness. If the color bleeds, have your bedspread dry cleaned.

- If it is safe to wash your bedspread, we advise you to wash it before
  it becomes heavily soiled. Treat spots and stains with a spray prewash
  product or liquid detergent.

- Use a large commercial washing machine for oversized bedspreads. An
  overcrowded washer won't clean very well.

- Dry bedspreads across several clotheslines or in a large commercial dryer.

Blankets

- Blankets are made of many different fibers and blends, but most of them are washable by hand or machine. Some wool blankets can be machine washed, some cannot. Check the care label and follow the manufacturer's instructions.

- Air blankets on a clothesline periodically to refresh them.

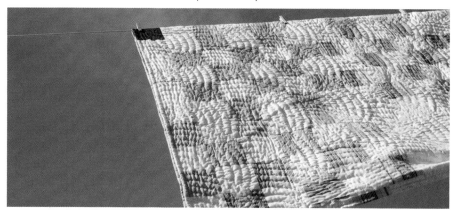

- Before you wash a blanket, mend or replace bindings and treat spots and stains. Use a large commercial washer to wash large blankets. Fill the washer with water and put in the detergent so it can completely dissolve before you add the blanket. Use a gentle (delicate) wash cycle; long periods of agitation will mat blanket fibers. Also avoid overcrowding the machine. A fabric softener will increase a blanket's fluffiness and reduce static electricity.

- When washing cotton or washable wool blankets, add 2 cups vinegar to the rinse cycle. This will help remove soap and make blankets soft and fluffy.

Down-Filled Comforters & Quilts

- The down filling in some comforters and quilts is held in place by tufts of yarn or by stitched-through patterns. Most down-filled comforters and quilts are washable, but some older ones are too fragile to be cleaned at home.

- Follow the manufacturer's care instructions if they are available. Test older comforters and quilts for colorfastness by wetting an inconspicuous spot with the detergent solution you plan to use and blotting the area with a white blotter.

- If comforters or quilts are in good condition, machine wash and dry them. Use cold wash water and rinse water and all-purpose detergent. Fragile down comforters and quilts should be hand washed in the bathtub or a deep laundry tub.

- Drape the wet comforter or quilt over several clotheslines to allow excess moisture to drip out; reposition it periodically. If the comforter or quilt is strong enough to be dried in a clothes dryer, preheat the dryer to a low temperature and include a pair of clean, dry sneakers to help fluff the down. The dryer can also be set on air dry (no heat) to dry the quilt.

Wool-, Cotton-, & Synthetic-Filled Comforters & Quilts

- Most cotton- or polyester-filled comforters and quilts are washable, but older quilts may be too delicate to withstand washing.

- Some newer wool-filled or wool-covered comforters and quilts can be washed at home; others should be dry-cleaned.

- Follow the manufacturer's care instructions if they are available. Test old quilts and comforters for colorfastness before attempting to wash them by wetting a small area with the detergent solution and blotting it with a white blotter.

- Clean patchwork quilts with the method that is appropriate for the most delicate fabric in the quilt. Never attempt to wash silk- or velvet-covered quilts and comforters.

- For small- to medium-size quilts and comforters, use your home washing machine. For large quilts, use a commercial washer. Let quilts and comforters soak in the machine for about 10 minutes before starting them through a short, gentle (delicate) washing cycle.

- Hand wash and line-dry old or fragile quilts and all quilts with cotton batting. Machine washing is too harsh and can cause cotton batting to bunch up. Use a bathtub or deep laundry tub, and allow the soap or detergent to dissolve in the wash water before adding the quilt.

Mattress & Box Springs

- Vacuum mattresses and box springs, and turn the mattress over and around end-to-end to ensure even wear. Use an upholstery attachment on your vacuum cleaner, and work carefully around any buttons on your mattress. Remove dust and blanket fluff from the edges of the box spring with your vacuum brush attachment.

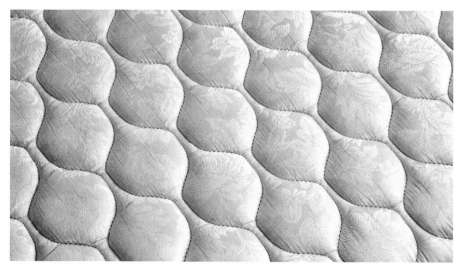

- Cover mattresses with quilted or rubberized pads that can be quickly washed when they become soiled.

- Remove spots and stains promptly, but do not allow the mattress to become excessively wet when you spot clean it.

- Do not make the bed until the mattress is completely dry.

Pillows

- Protect your pillows with a zip-on cotton or polyester cover, which you can wash regularly. Refresh pillows by airing them near an open window or hanging them on a clothesline outside.

- Kapok is the silky covering of seeds from the ceiba tree; pillows with this stuffing need frequent airing but cannot be washed.

- Fluff down and feather pillows when you make your bed to get rid of accumulated dust and to redistribute the filling. Before you wash a feather or down pillow, make sure it has no holes or ripped seams. Machine or hand wash feather and down pillows in cool water with cold-water, light-duty detergent. Wash two pillows at a time or add a couple of bath towels to balance the load. If the fabric is worn or the pillow is heavily stuffed, wash the feathers and ticking separately. Secure the feathers in a large muslin bag and stitch the opening closed.

- Dry down and feather pillows in the dryer on the low-heat setting. Including a pair of clean, dry tennis shoes in the dryer will help distribute the down as it dries.

- Hand wash and line-dry foam pillows. Change the hanging position hourly to dry the filling evenly. Never put a foam pillow in the dryer.

- For polyester-filled pillows, read the care-instruction tags; some polyester-filled pillows are washable, but some are not. Machine or hand wash polyester-filled pillows in warm water with an all-purpose detergent. A front-loading tumble washer rather than a top-loading machine works best for polyester pillows. Dry the pillows in the dryer on a moderate heat setting.

Laundry

When we think about laundry, we often imagine snow-white sheets billowing in the breeze, shirts with no telltale stains or rings around the collars, glimmering little-league uniforms, and baby-soft, sweet-smelling piles of neatly folded clothes. The reality of laundry is less exciting. But if you don't keep up with the laundry, you won't have anything to wear. Since you have to do it, make it as easy as you can. We're here to help speed you through piles of laundry, with guidelines and tips on how to care for everything from your favorite sweatshirt to your best silk blouse.

Your Laundry Room/The Laundromat

- Opening a detergent box with a pour spout can be hazardous to your fingernails. Use a "church key" bottle opener—the flat end will probably work best.

- Freshen laundry hampers by sprinkling baking soda over dirty clothes as they await washing.

- To mask the odor of dirty laundry, keep a dryer sheet in the bottom of your laundry basket, bag, or hamper.

- Make an impromptu garment bag: Cut a hole in the center of the bottom seam of a trash bag (unscented, twist-tie variety). Turn it upside down and place over a hanger.

- Don't lug all those boxes and bottles to the Laundromat. Instead, put a load of laundry into a pillowcase, then pour in the right amount of powdered detergent and bleach for the load. Just dump it all into the washer!

- Save energy (your own!) en route to the Laundromat by premeasuring detergents or other products into plastic tubs or plastic bags.

Understanding Fabric Care Labels

The first step toward doing your laundry quickly and efficiently is to know what an item is made of and the best way to care for it. Most garments and many other fabric items manufactured and sold in the United States have permanently attached care labels. These labels are also required on garments made of suede and leather. They can be of enormous help in determining exactly how you should remove stains and clean an item.

- Certain information is not included on care labels. Neither the manufacturer nor the retailer is required to inform a consumer that a certain fabric will shrink.

- The label assumes that the purchaser knows that an item labeled "hand wash" should be washed in lukewarm water and that all nonwhite articles should not be treated with chlorine bleach.

- Another important piece of information contained on fabric care labels is the fiber content of the material. This is especially important with blends. These fabrics are combinations of fibers, such as cotton and wool, cotton and polyester, or wool and acrylic. Blends should be cared for in the same way as the fiber with the highest percentage in the blend. For example, a blend of 60 percent cotton and 40 percent polyester should be cleaned as though it were 100 percent cotton. However, when you remove spots and stains, you should follow procedures recommended for the most delicate fiber in the blend. For example, to remove stains from a blend of cotton and silk, use the procedure recommended for silk. If after such treatment the stain is still apparent, follow the procedure for cotton, the most durable fiber in this blend.

Cotton

Cotton fabric is strong, long-wearing, and absorbent. It will shrink and wrinkle unless it is given special treatment. Cotton is often blended with other fibers or treated with a finish to make it wrinkle-resistant. It is available in a wide variety of weights and textures, from denim or corduroy to percale.

- Machine wash and tumble-dry cotton fabrics, using a water temperature ranging from cold to hot, depending on the manufacturer's care instructions, and an all-purpose detergent.

- If needed, a chlorine bleach can be used on white or colorfast cotton unless a fabric finish has been applied. Do not use more than the recommended amount of bleach; this can damage the fibers.

- We recommend that you use fabric softener to improve softness and to reduce wrinkling. But fabric softener makes cotton less absorbent and should not be used on towels, washcloths, or diapers.

- Pretreat oil-based spots and stains with a prewash.

- Wash and shrink cotton fabrics before using them for home sewing.

- Iron cotton with a hot iron for best results and use spray starch or spray sizing to restore its crisp appearance.

Linen

Pure linen fabric wrinkles easily, so many manufacturers make linen blends or add wrinkle-resistant finishes to overcome this problem. Linen is absorbent and comfortable to wear, but it can crack or show wear at the seams, along the creases, and at the finished edges of the garment.

- Machine wash and tumble-dry linen. An all-purpose detergent is the best cleaning agent, and chlorine bleach can be used on white linen, following the manufacturer's recommended amount so as not to damage the fabric.

- Linen can also be dry cleaned. It should be pressed with a hot iron while it is still slightly damp for the best results.

Silk

Silk is a delight to wear, but it requires special care. Most silk garments are marked "dry-clean only." However, some silk can be washed by hand. A piece of silk fabric that you are going to make into a garment should first be washed by hand.

- We suggest that you always test a corner of the fabric for colorfastness before washing a whole piece of silk. Some dyed silk will bleed.

- Use a hair shampoo containing protein and warm or cool water for hand washing; the protein in the shampoo feeds the protein in the silk.

- Handle washable silk gently during washing; never twist or wring it.

- Hang silk out of direct sunlight to drip-dry.

- Press silk while it is still damp with a warm iron (below 275 degrees Fahrenheit) or use a steam iron.

- To remove stains from washable white or light-colored silk, use only oxygen bleach or mix 1 part hydrogen peroxide (3 percent) to 8 parts water.

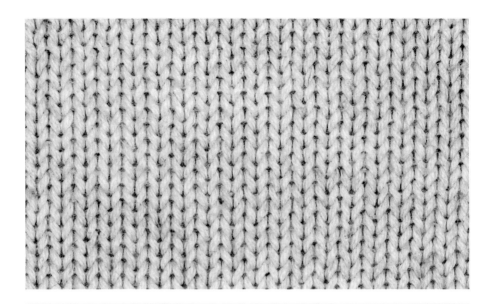

Wool

Wool fabric is highly resilient, absorbent, and sheds wrinkles well, but wool will shrink and mat if it's exposed to heat and rubbing. Popular in both knit and woven fabrics, the textures of wool fabrics range from fine wool crepe and jersey to felt and mohair.

- Treat spots and stains on wool fabrics with solvent-based spot removers. Clean felt by wiping it with a dry sponge. For a more thorough treatment, hold the material over steam from a teakettle, and brush lightly with a dry sponge or lint-free cloth to smooth the surface.

- Wool should always be dry-cleaned unless it is specifically marked "washable."

- Use light-duty detergent in cold water to wash wool. Allow the article to soak for a few minutes before starting the washing process. Handle woolens carefully when they are wet to avoid stretching. Machine washing is appropriate only if the care label indicates that it is, and then use only cold water and the gentle cycle.

- Remove excess moisture by rolling a wool article in a towel, then block it into shape and dry it on a flat surface. Only machine-dry woolens if the manufacturer's instructions recommend it.

- Press wool with a hot iron, using lots of steam. Cover the article with a damp cloth or chemically treated press cloth. Allow the garment to dry thoroughly before storing it.

Acetate

Acetate is made from cellulose and has a silk-like appearance. Closely related to rayon, it has good body and drapes well. Taffeta, satin, crepe, brocade, and double knits often contain acetate. It is not very absorbent or colorfast, and acetate loses its strength when it is wet.

- Hand wash acetate carefully in warm water, using a light-duty detergent, if the care label specifies that the article is washable; otherwise have it dry-cleaned. Do not soak colored items or wash them with white articles. Add fabric softener to the rinse water to reduce wrinkles.

- Line-dry acetate away from heat or direct sunlight. Press at the coolest setting, on the wrong side, while the article is damp. Use a press cloth when pressing the right side of the fabric.

- Nail-polish remover and perfumes will permanently damage acetate.

Among the frequently asked questions to 3M's product information line is this:

"Can duct tape be used to secure the duct from the household dryer to the outdoors?"

ANSWER:

No. The company does not recommend it because the temperatures may be hotter than 200 degrees F (93 degrees C), which is the maximum temperature duct tape can take.

Acrylic

Many acrylic weaves resemble wool's softness, bulk, and fluffiness. Acrylics are wrinkle-resistant and usually are machine washable. Often acrylic fibers are blended with wool or polyester fibers. Acrylic's biggest drawback is its tendency to pill. Blends will do this less than pure acrylic.

- Dry-clean acrylic garments or wash them by hand or in the machine.

- Pretreat oil-based stains, and turn garments inside out before laundering to reduce pilling.

- Wash delicate items by hand in warm water, gently squeezing out the water.

- Machine wash sturdy articles with an all-purpose detergent, and tumble-dry at low temperatures.

- If the fabric is labeled "colorfast," it can be bleached with either chlorine or oxygen bleach. We've found that adding fabric softener to the rinse water every third or fourth time an article is washed reduces static electricity.

- Press at a moderate temperature setting, using steam.

Nylon

Nylon fabrics are extremely strong, lightweight, smooth, and lustrous. They are also nonabsorbent and have excellent abrasion- and wrinkle-resistance. Often combined with spandex, nylon knits are very stretchy but hold and recover their original shape. Available in many textures, nylon is used to make all kinds of items, including lingerie, carpets, rainwear, and tents.

- Always follow the manufacturer's cleaning instructions.

- Pretreat oil-based stains on nylon.

- Machine wash sturdy articles in warm water with an all-purpose detergent.

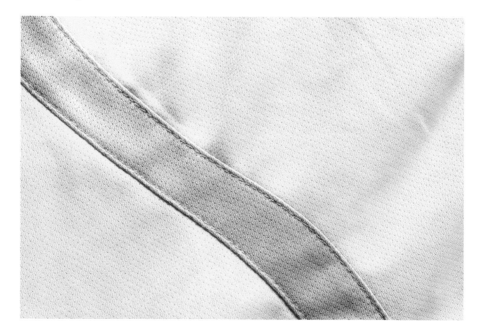

- Hand wash lingerie and hosiery, using warm water and light-duty detergent, or machine wash in a mesh bag to prevent stretching or tearing. Do not launder white nylon with colored fabrics of any kind.

- Use a chlorine bleach only if a nylon article is colorfast, and use fabric softener to reduce static electricity.

- Tumble-dry nylon at a low temperature setting.

- Press at a cool temperature setting.

Polyester

Polyester fabrics are strong, resilient, wrinkle-resistant, colorfast, and crisp. They hold pleats and creases well, but they are also nonabsorbent, attract and hold oil-based stains, may pill when rubbed, and may yellow with age. Polyester is used for clothing and filling; some bed linens and towels are also made from polyester blends.

- Polyester can be safely dry-cleaned or machine washed.

- Pretreat oil-based stains with prewash or all-purpose liquid detergent.

- Turn polyester-knit garments inside out before washing to prevent snags.

- Machine wash polyester in warm water using an all-purpose detergent, and tumble-dry at a low temperature setting. Use a chlorine bleach if necessary. Using a fabric softener will reduce static electricity.

- Do not overdry polyester; this will cause gradual shrinkage. Press polyester fabrics at a moderate temperature setting or use steam.

Rayon

Rayon is a strong, absorbent fabric, but it tends to lose its strength when it is wet. It is used for drapery and upholstery fabrics as well as for clothing.

- Dry-clean rayon or wash it by hand unless it is labeled "machine washable."

- For hand wash, use lukewarm water with a light-duty detergent. Squeeze moisture out gently when washing rayon fabrics by hand.

- Machine wash rayon in warm water on a gentle cycle with a light-duty detergent.

- Chlorine bleach can be used on rayon unless it has been treated with a resin finish.

- Drip-dry and press rayon on the wrong side with an iron at a medium temperature setting while the fabric is damp.

Triacetate

Triacetate resembles acetate, but it is less sensitive to heat. This allows triacetate to be creased and crisply pleated. Triacetate is often a component in jersey, textured knits, and taffeta.

- Pleated garments can be hand or machine washed in cold water.

- Set the gentle cycle to agitate for 3 minutes. Drip-dry permanently pleated garments, or air-dry them in dryer.

- Most triacetate articles can be machine washed with an all-purpose detergent in hot or warm water. Tumble- or line-dry triacetate. Press, if necessary, using a hot temperature setting.

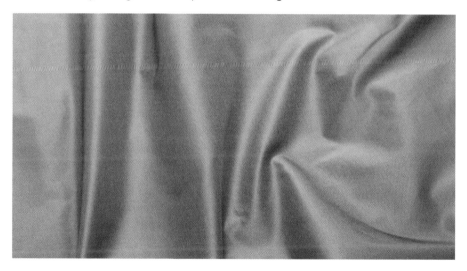

Spandex

Spandex is a lightweight fiber that resembles rubber in durability. It has good stretch and recovery, and it is resistant to damage from sunlight, abrasion, and oils. Always blended with other fibers, spandex provides the stretch in waistbands, foundation garments, swimwear, and dancewear.

- Pretreat oil-based stains.

- Hand or machine wash spandex-blend garments in warm water using an all-purpose detergent.

- Do not wash white spandex with colored fabrics of any kind. Use only oxygen or sodium-perborate bleach. Rinse thoroughly.

- Line-dry or tumble-dry garments made with spandex at a low temperature setting.

- Press clothing that contains spandex rapidly, if needed, using a low temperature setting.

Laundry Techniques

You could jam all your dirty laundry in the washing machine, run it through whatever wash cycle happens to be programmed, and hope for the best. This method may leave your sweater doll-sized or turn your white silk shirt pink, but it's quick—if you don't count the time you'll spend replacing your ruined clothes. Doing your laundry properly will take more time. Your clothes will last longer and look better if you pay careful attention to sorting, pretreating, water temperature, machine cycle, and the right laundry products for each particular fabric.

- Properly sorting the laundry is the first step to a clean wash and helps to keep your clothes, linens, and other household items looking their best through repeated washings.

- **Color:** First sort the laundry by color. Put all the white or predominantly white articles in one pile, the light colors and pastels in another pile, and the bright and dark-colored items into a third. Then separate the dark pile into two piles: one for colorfast items and one for noncolorfast items.

- **Degree of soil:** Separate each pile into three smaller piles: lightly soiled, moderately soiled, and heavily soiled.

- **Compatible loads:** Now you have up to 12 various-sized piles of laundry. Combine or divide the piles to come up with compatible, washer-sized loads. The following hints will help you with your final sorting:

- Combine white and light-colored items that have similar degrees of soil into the same pile.

- Combine noncolorfast items with similarly colored colorfast items with the same degree of soil.

- Create a separate pile for delicate items that must be hand washed.

- Separate white synthetic articles, and wash them only with other white fabrics.

- Separate synthetics, blends, and permanent-press fabrics from natural-fiber fabrics without special finishes.

- Separate items made from fabrics that produce lint, such as chenille robes and bath towels, from fabrics that attract lint, such as corduroy, knits, synthetics, and permanent press.

Preparing the Wash

- Know the fiber content and finishes of fabrics so you can select the proper water temperature and cleaning products.

- Save care information so you can follow the recommended cleaning procedures.

- Close all zippers, hook all hooks, and button all buttons.

- Turn pockets inside out to get rid of debris.

- Remove nonwashable trim or decorations and pins or buckles that might make holes or snag other articles in the wash.

- Tie or buckle all belts and sashes to prevent tangling.

- Mend seams, tears, holes, or loose hems to prevent further damage during the wash cycle.

- Turn sweaters and corduroy garments inside out to prevent pilling and to combat their tendency to collect lint.

- Pretreat spots, stains, and heavily soiled items with prewash spot-and-stain remover, liquid detergent, a paste made from granular soap or detergent, a bar of soap, or a presoak solution.

- Remove the smell of cigarette smoke from clothes by soaking them in a solution of 4 tablespoons baking soda and 1 quart water before washing.

- Use equal parts water and vinegar to pretreat common stains on clothing. Spray mixture on stains before washing to give an extra boost.

- Pretreat collar stains on shirts with cornstarch. Dampen collar, rub a little in, and launder as usual.

Prewash Spot-and-Stain Removers

- While soaps and detergents can be worked directly into spots and heavily soiled areas before you put the laundry into the washer, a special product designed just for removing spots and stains is more convenient to use. Called prewash spot-and-stain removers, these aerosols or pump sprays are excellent for spot treating stubborn soil, especially grease marks on synthetic fabrics.

- Treat the stain while it is still fresh. Saturate the soiled area completely, then lightly rub the fabric together to work the prewash product into the fibers.

- Some prewash products can damage the exterior finish of your washer and dryer, so be careful where you spray them.

Presoaks

- Granular presoak products containing enzymes break down some stubborn stains such as milk, blood, baby formula, chocolate, gravy, fruits and vegetables, and grass. Presoaks are not effective on rust, ink, oil, or grease.

- Following the manufacturer's directions, mix a solution in a large sink or in the washer. Before adding the soiled laundry, make sure that the presoak has dissolved thoroughly.

- Soak clothes for the recommended length of time; an overnight soak is suitable for articles that look dull and dingy.

- Do not soak dark- and light-colored fabrics together for long periods of time; this can cause colors to run.

- Wash the laundry as usual after using a presoak.

- You can use presoaks for diaper-pail solutions and as detergent boosters.

Laundry Products

Most commercial laundry preparations are designed to be used in washing machines, but some can be used for both hand and machine washing. Read the label carefully before purchasing any product to make sure it is the right one for the job you want it to do. When you use a laundry product, follow the directions precisely and measure accurately.

- **Water Conditioners:** The amount and type of chemicals and minerals dissolved in water determines whether it is hard or soft. The condition of the water affects the cleaning potential of laundry products: The softer the water, the more effective it is for cleaning. Determine the hardness of your water so you will know if you need to condition it for effective cleaning.

- Hard water leaves a residue on articles you launder; this is known as washing film. To soften water, the minerals must be removed or chemically locked up. Water that measures under four grains hardness per gallon will probably clean effectively, especially if a detergent rather than soap is used. You can soften hard water with a mechanical water softener that attaches to your home's water tank or by adding a water-conditioning product to the wash and rinse water.

- Follow the directions on product labels precisely.

- Wash flame-retardant items only in soft water.

- Use a water conditioner to remove previously formed washing film or soap/detergent buildup. You can also remove hard-water washing film from diapers, towels, or fabrics by soaking them in a solution of 1 cup white vinegar and 1 gallon water in a plastic container.

- Use a water softener if you use soap in hard water or if you use a phosphate-free detergent.

- **Detergents and Soaps:** Soap is a mixture of alkalis and fats that is a good cleaner in soft water, breaks down well in city sewer systems, and does not harm the environment. Soap is less effective in hard water, however, because it reacts with the high mineral content to form soap curd, which leaves a gray scum on clothing.

- Detergents are synthetic washing products derived from petroleum and other nonfatty materials. They are less affected by hard water than soap and have excellent cleaning power. Since detergents contain a wetting agent that lifts off dirt and agents that help to make hard water minerals inactive, they do not create scum.

- It was once common for detergents to contain phosphates, which are harmful to the environment because they promote an overgrowth of algae in water, but store-bought detergents today are phosphate-free. The cleaning ability of phosphate-free detergents is less effective in hard water and in cold-water washes than detergents that contain phosphates, and these detergents may cause excessive wear to some fabrics.

- Always follow the manufacturer's instructions for the amount of detergent to use, the proper wash cycle, and the recommended water temperature. Measure carefully, but use extra detergent for heavy and/or greasy soil, larger-than-normal loads, and warm- or cold-water washes.

- You may also need more than the manufacturer's recommended amount of detergent if you have hard water and when you use phosphate-free detergent. Adding 1 cup ammonia to the wash water will boost detergent effectiveness for heavily soiled or greasy wash loads.

- Use liquid detergents in cold-water washes for best results, or dissolve powder or granular detergents in 1 quart hot water, then add the solution to the cold wash water.

- **Bleach:** Bleach works with detergent or soap to remove stains and soil, whiten white items, and brighten the colors of some fabrics. It also acts as a mild disinfectant. The two basic types of laundry bleach are chlorine and oxygen. Common liquid chlorine bleach is the most effective and least expensive, but it cannot be used on all fabrics. Oxygen bleach is safer for all washable fabrics, resin-finished fibers, and most washable colors, but it is much less strong than chlorine bleach.

- Always give colored fabrics a colorfastness test before using any bleach by mixing 1 tablespoon chlorine bleach with 1/4 cup warm water or; 1 tablespoon oxygen bleach with 2 quarts hot water. Apply the solution to an inconspicuous place; wait a few minutes and check for a color change. If the color does not bleed, use the bleach according to the manufacturer's directions.

- Add diluted chlorine bleach to the wash water about five minutes after the wash cycle has begun or use the automatic bleach dispenser if your washer is equipped with one. Bleach clothes only in the wash cycle so the bleach can be completely removed during the rinse cycle. Hot water improves the performance of bleach.

- **Fabric Softeners:** Fabric softeners add softness and fluffiness, reduce static electricity on synthetics so they will not cling, help decrease lint, and make pressing easier. They are available in liquid, sheet, or solid form.

- Liquid fabric softener is added to the wash or rinse cycle; sheet and solid products are used in the dryer.

- Read the instructions for using a fabric softener to determine at what time in the laundering cycle to add it. Dilute liquid fabric softeners with water before adding them to the automatic fabric-softener dispenser or to the rinse.

- Fabric softener can stain fabric if it is poured or sprayed directly onto clothes or if it is used with a water conditioner. Sheet fabric softeners will stain polyester articles if they are used in the dryer when these fabrics are drying.

- If you stain an item with fabric softener, rub the stained area with liquid detergent or a prewash spot-and-stain remover and rewash the article.

Getting the Best Results from Your Washing Machine

- Do not overload the machine; garments should not pile up past the top of the agitator.

- Mix small and large items in each load for the best circulation, and distribute the load evenly around the wash basket.

- Loading the washer to full capacity each time you wash will save time and energy. But don't be tempted to throw your dark bath towels in a bleach load or your sweaters in a permanent-press load just to fill it.

- Add 1/2 cup vinegar to the rinse cycle of your wash to soften clothes.

The correct water temperature(s) for a load of wash varies according to the kinds of fabric being washed and the amount of soil. Use the following chart to help you select the proper wash and rinse temperature settings.

Type of Load	Wash Temperature	Rinse Temperature
White and light-colored cottons and linens Diapers Heavily soiled permanent-press and wash-and-wear fabrics All other greasy or heavily soiled wash	130° F.-150° F. (hot)	warm or cold
Dark colors Lightly and moderately soiled permanent-press and wash-and-wear fabrics Some woven or knit synthetic fabrics (see care label) Some washable woolens (see care label) Any other moderately soiled wash	100° F.-110° F. (warm)	cold
Noncolorfast fabrics Some washable woolens (see care label) Some woven or knit synthetic fabrics (see care label) Fragile items Bright colors Any lightly soiled wash	80° F.-100° F. (cold)	cold

- Use enough water to provide good circulation, but do not use so much that you waste water and energy. Most machines have a water-level control, and you should adjust this control to match each load you wash. Refer to the manufacturer's instructions for this information.

- Select the type of cycle according to the kind of load and the degree of soil. Follow these guidelines, using a longer cycle for heavily soiled laundry.

Type of Load	Cycle
Sturdy white and colorfast items	Normal
Sturdy noncolorfast items	Normal
Sturdy permanent-press and wash-and-wear fabrics	Permanent-press
Delicate fabrics and knits	Gentle or delicate

Dry-Clean Only?

- Never use vinegar on dry-clean-only fabrics. It's always a good idea to test the fabric for colorfastness before treating a stain.

- Even if the tag says "dry-clean only," some items can be cleaned with a solution of 4 tablespoons baking soda in a sink of cold water. Test for colorfastness first.

Washing by Hand

- We recommend that you never disregard the "hand wash only" label even when you're in a hurry.

- Sort hand wash in the same way you sort machine wash. Separate the clothes into piles by color, putting white and light colors together, dark and noncolorfast items into separate piles.

- Pretreat stains and heavily soiled areas with prewash spot-and-stain remover or by rubbing liquid detergent into the area.

- Use light-duty soap or detergent and dissolve it in warm or cool wash water before adding the clothes. Submerge the articles in the water and let them soak for 3 to 5 minutes. Gently squeeze the suds through the fabric, being careful not to rub, twist, or wring excessively. Rinse articles thoroughly in cool water until the water runs clear. Add a few drops of fabric softener to the last rinse if desired.

- Hang blouses, dresses, scarves, and lingerie to drip-dry. The shower is a good place for this. Use towels to blot excess moisture from sweaters, stockings, panties, and bras. Hang these items to dry only if the weight of the water will not stretch them out of shape; otherwise, dry them on a towel on a flat surface.

- When washing delicate items by hand, follow garment's care instructions and add 1 or 2 tablespoons vinegar to the last rinse to help remove soap residue.

- Eliminate the stale smell in stored-away hand-washables by soaking them in a solution of 4 tablespoons baking soda and 1 quart water. Rinse well, squeeze, then air-dry.

Machine Drying

- Shake out each article before placing it in the dryer to speed the drying time and cut down on wrinkles. Do not overload the dryer; this will cause uneven drying and excessive wrinkling.

- Remove items from the dryer as soon as it stops, and hang or fold them to keep them from getting wrinkled.

- Dry clothes until they are "almost dry" rather than "bone dry" if you are going to iron them.

- Clean the lint filter after each use of the dryer.

- Lint won't stick to your clothes while they're tumbling in the dryer if you toss in a pair of pantyhose with them.

- A few tennis balls tumbling around in the dryer will be somewhat noisy... but very effective for reducing static cling. Toss them in with a load of clothes and set the dryer on low heat.

Line-Drying

- If you are going to the trouble to hang your clothes outside to dry, make sure that your clothespins and clotheslines are clean and free of rust. You can wash plastic clothespins in mild soap and warm water in an automatic clothes washer, using a mesh bag. Wash wooden clothespins in a hot dish-washing-detergent solution. Use plastic rope or plastic-coated wire for your clothesline, and wipe it with a damp cloth before using it.

- Attach items to the clothesline by their most sturdy edges.

- Smooth the clothes as you hang them, running your fingers down seams and along the front, collar, and cuff edges. Dry white and light-colored items in the sun and bright-colored items in the shade.

- Hang pants by the cuffs and let their weight reduce wrinkles.

- Cut the fingers off a pair of cotton gloves, then slip the "fingers" over the arms of a weathered clothespin. They'll prevent marks on your clothes.

- Drop a spoon into each leg of a pair of pantyhose or another thin garment to keep them from wrapping around the clothesline on a windy day.

- Bring in clothes as soon as they dry. Bright sun and extreme cold can weaken fibers.

Troubleshooting: Yellowed Fabric & Dye Problems

- If your good ol' black cotton T-shirts have faded to dark brown or eggplant from frequent washings, add 1 cup strong Lipton tea to the rinse cycle next time. They'll be restored to their original glory.

- Whiten yellowed linens by dropping 1 or 2 denture cleanser tablets in a tub of warm water and soaking the fabric overnight.

- Any colored clothing item that has dulled can be brightened by soaking it in 1 gallon warm water and 1 cup vinegar. Follow this with a clear water rinse.

- Boil yellowed cotton or linen fabrics in a mixture of water, 1 tablespoon salt, and 1/4 cup baking soda. Soak for 1 hour, then launder as usual.

- Bleach soiled handkerchiefs by soaking them for a few hours in a solution of warm water and 1 tablespoon McCormick Cream of Tartar. Soak especially dingy hankies for about an hour in a sink of water with 1 tablespoon cream of tartar and 2 teaspoons Tide laundry detergent. Wash as usual.

- If you just can't get those dingy whites clean, don't discard them. Strong, hot Lipton tea is the perfect dye for natural-fiber fabric or yarn. Soak the material until it is a shade darker than desired (as it dries, it becomes lighter). Rinse in clear, cold water; allow to air-dry.

- Herbal teas can also dye fabrics. Go bold or subtle as you use, for example, hibiscus for red tones or licorice for soft brown. Always experiment on fabric scraps to get the results you want.

Troubleshooting: Stains

- Equal parts bleach and milk can take stains out of old linens. Make a small quantity of the solution, dip a cotton ball in it, and gently dab the stains. When the spots are gone, launder as usual. This treatment also works on discoloration lines that form on the folds of long-stored linens.

- For tough stains, including mildew, make a thin paste of lemon juice and salt. Apply to the stain, set the item in the sun to dry, then wash as usual.

- Here's another method to get rid of mildew: A mixture of salt, distilled white vinegar, and water should remove mildew stains on most fabrics. Use up to full-strength vinegar if mildew is extensive.

- To remove a food stain (whether fresh or dried-on) from a washable item of clothing, use club soda. First, blot the spill by pressing lightly with a paper towel. Then sponge the fabric with club soda and launder as usual.

- Remove a wine spill from cotton fabric by immediately sprinkling stained area with enough salt to soak up liquid. Soak fabric for 1 hour in cold water, then launder as usual.

- A red wine stain yields to club soda. If the spot is still wet, blot it with a paper towel. Pour on a generous amount of club soda; rub gently with another paper towel or a sponge. Repeat if necessary.

- To remove tough juice stains, dilute lemon juice or distilled white vinegar with water. Soak the stain in this solution, then wash as usual.

- Brand-new coffee or tea drips should be removed easily with lots of cold water on a damp cloth (if fabric is not dry-clean only). For coffee or tea stains that have set, soak item in a solution of 1 part vinegar and 2 parts water, then hang in the sun to dry.

- Those hard-to-fix bleach spots on clothes might be fixable with a crayon. Pick a matching color, warm the fabric with an iron, and color the spot. Cover it with wax paper and iron on low to set the color.

- To remove a bloodstain, dampen the area with water and rub with baking soda. Follow by dabbing with hydrogen peroxide until the stain is gone. Test for colorfastness first.

- You can also get rid of a bloodstain by applying a paste of cornstarch and water to the stain right away. Let dry, then brush off. Repeat if necessary. This works on clothing and linens.

- Clean a fresh bloodstain with hydrogen peroxide. Dab on the peroxide, then blot off, repeating as necessary. Test a hidden area first to be sure the fabric is colorfast.

- A fresh bloodstain should disappear easily if it is immediately covered with salt and blotted with cold water. Keep adding fresh water and blotting until stain is gone.

- Chocolate stains melt away in the face of undiluted ammonia. Scrub the stained area, then wash as usual.

- Revive grass-stained clothes or sneakers with molasses. Rub a little molasses into any stains; let sit overnight. Wash item with a mild soap— not laundry detergent.

- Remove severe grass stains from white clothes by soaking in undiluted vinegar for a half hour before washing.

- Rub baking soda into polyester fabrics to remove a grease spot. Brush off, and the stain should be gone.

- A grease stain can sometimes be removed by rubbing baby powder or cornstarch into it. Allow the powder or corn starch to sit for an hour or more to soak up the grease, then brush off and wash as usual. If stain remains, repeat until it's gone.

- To remove a fresh grease spill on fabric, cover with salt or corn meal and allow it to absorb as much of the mess as possible. Repeat until spot is gone. Brush off and launder.

- Double-knit fabrics can be a special stain challenge when it comes to grease. Add 1/2 teaspoon salt to a small dish of ammonia and dab mixture directly onto grease spot. Let sit, then wash as usual.

- Try covering a fresh gravy stain with salt and letting it absorb as much of the grease as possible. A stubborn stain may require dabbing and blotting with a solution of equal parts ammonia and vinegar until it disappears.

- Pour Pepsi or club soda directly on a grease spot. Let it sit for a few minutes to loosen the stain, then wash as usual.

- Remove grease from suede by dipping a cloth in vinegar and gently sponging stain. Let dry completely, then use a fine brush to restore nap in suede.

- Clean suede with baking soda applied with a soft brush. Let it sit, then brush it off.

- Remove an ink stain from leather by laying the item flat and sprinkling baking soda on the stain. Leave on until ink is absorbed, brush off, and repeat if necessary.

- Ink stains or scuff marks on suede clothing or shoes can be removed, or at least minimized, with fine-grit 3M sandpaper. Sand with a light touch, then use an old toothbrush or a nailbrush to restore the nap afterward.

- A lipstick stain on silk sounds like an automatic bill from the dry cleaner. Try this method instead. Place a piece of clear tape or masking tape on the spot, then pull it off. If some of the lipstick remains, sprinkle on some baby powder or crushed chalk. With a clean cloth, dab until both the powder and the lipstick vanish.

- Oil stain got you stumped? Dip a wedge of lime in salt and rub the spot. Launder as usual.

- Conquer rust stains with this treatment. Wet the stained area with lemon juice; hold it directly over the steam from a pot of boiling water for a few minutes. Rinse well.

  Make a thin paste of distilled white vinegar and salt and spread paste on a rust stain in fabric. Lay item out in the sun to bleach it. Alternatively, apply paste, stretch fabric over a large kettle, and pour boiling water through stained area. In both cases, allow item to dry, then check stain. Run item through the rinse cycle in your washing machine and check stain again. Repeat treatment if any stain remains.

- To remove a rust mark on fabric, dampen the spot and rub cream of tartar into it. Wait 1 hour, then wash as usual. Repeat if necessary.

- Those yellow stains in the armpits and around the collars of your favorite white T-shirts aren't a sign that you're sweating too much or not cleaning properly. These areas are just harder to get clean and are made up of more than just old perspiration and dirt. Plus, if you have hard water, the deodorant residue (and soap and perspiration) won't wash out properly. Here's one method for attacking these problem stains: Mix 1 quart water with 4 tablespoons salt. Sponge this mixture onto stained areas; repeat until stains disappear. Launder as usual.

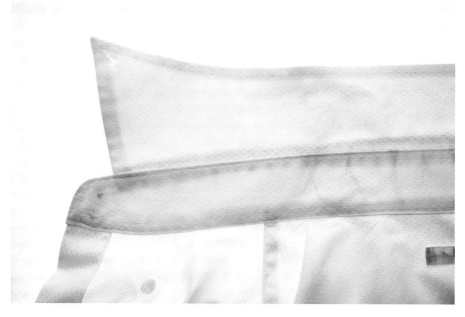

- Aspirin can remove perspiration stains from white fabrics. Dissolve 2 tablets in 1/2 cup of warm water and apply to the stain. Let it sit for about 2 hours before laundering.

- For perspiration stains, scrub on a paste of baking soda and water; let sit for 1 hour, then launder as usual.

- Try soaking white shirts and T-shirts in undiluted vinegar to get rid of yellow stains in the armpits and around the collar. Let the item sit in the vinegar for 15 to 20 minutes, then launder as usual.

- Treat stubborn perspiration stains around the collar with a paste of 4 tablespoons baking soda and 1/4 cup water. Rub in, add a little distilled white vinegar to the collar, and wash.

- Remove candle wax from fabric such as clothing or table linens by putting a paper towel or a brown paper bag over the spot. Press with an iron on a low heat setting (keep the iron in one place) for several seconds. The wax will be absorbed by the paper and the iron will remain clean.

- Clean leather with a mixture of 1 cup boiled linseed oil and 1 cup vinegar. Carefully apply to any spots with a soft cloth. Let dry.

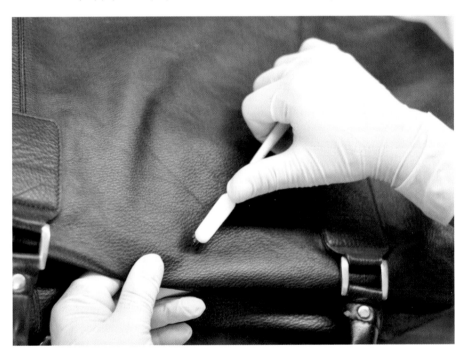

- A toothbrush is a wonderful laundry-day tool. To remove dried stains, put the garment on a flat surface, hold a piece of paper next to the stain, and gently brush the dried material onto the paper. Some stains, such as dried mud, are removed completely; others will have some residue that should come out during the regular wash cycle.

Clothing and Accessories

Doing your laundry isn't the only thing you can do to maintain your clothes. In this section we'll discuss some easy ways and quick fixes that will help your clothes last longer.

Clothing

- When you buy a new garment, dab the center of each button with clear nail enamel to seal the threads. The buttons will stay on longer.

- Put a stop to a run in your pantyhose by dabbing the ends of the run with clear nail enamel.

- Paint the edges of a fraying garment with clear nail enamel.

- Keep buckles from chipping or tarnishing by painting them with clear nail enamel. This also helps keep buckles shiny.

- Put a dab of clear nail enamel over the knot on a small ribbon to keep it from coming untied.

- To attach buttons more securely, sew them on with dental floss instead of thread. Just color the floss with a matching marker or crayon.

- Using a Q-tips cotton swab, apply a bit of extra virgin olive oil to the teeth of a stuck zipper. Slowly work the tab down until it's free.

- You can replace a missing zipper tab with a paper clip or a safety pin. Dress it up with a piece of ribbon or yarn or a dollop of paint.

- Fix a falling hem in a pinch with a length of duct tape. The tape is especially suited for heavy fabrics such as denim.

- You're all dressed up. You do have someplace to go. Unfortunately, you also have pet hair and lint on your outfit, and there's no lint remover in sight. Not to worry. Grab a roll of duct tape and cut a strip of tape about 5 inches long. Wrap it around your hand, adhesive side out, and roll it over your clothing until all the offending particles are gone. Make sure you aren't wiping the tape across the fabric; on some garments, it may mess up the nap.

- A rip in your ski pants or jacket can leave you cold, quite literally. Don't panic or pay exorbitant prices in the lodge shop to replace the item; just cut a length of duct tape a bit longer than the rip. Position the tape inside the rip, sticky side out. Join the two sides of the ripped fabric so they meet in the middle. Carefully press onto the tape.

Accessories

- Need a place to store your belts? Roll them up and place them in an empty coffee can. (Tip: A clear lid will make it easy to find the right belt.) These containers will keep your belts from creasing, and the easy access won't "waist" your time.

- Neatly store scarves in a dresser drawer using empty cores from rolls of toilet tissue or paper towels (cut in half). Stand them up in the drawer and tuck a folded scarf into each one.

In Your Closet

- Preserve space in your closet by hanging your scarves through plastic six-pack rings from soda cans. Attach the rings to a hanger using twist ties or clear tape.

- If a good pair of pants has been in the closet, on a regular hanger, for a while, there's likely an obvious, ugly crease from the hanger. Next time, cut an old paper towel tube lengthwise and place it over the bottom of the hanger. (Cut the ends of the tube to shorten if necessary.) Tape the tube back together to make sure it doesn't fall off the hanger. Hang your pants over the protective tube—good-bye, creases!

- Garments falling off their hangers? Before you hang a garment, put a rubber band on each end of the hanger.

- To keep spaghetti straps from slipping off wire hangers, use paper clips to attach them.

Jewelry Care

- Don't let it go down the drain: When cleaning your good jewelry, put a tea strainer over the sink drain.

- Dissolve 2 Alka-Seltzer tablets in a glass of water and use to soak dull or tarnished jewelry. Let soak for only 2 minutes, then rub dry.

- Extra virgin olive oil and vegetable oil each make a good cleaner for pearls. Just dab a little of either on each pearl, then wipe dry with a soft cloth.

- To clean a diamond ring, use Crest toothpaste on an old toothbrush. Scrub gently, rinse, dry, and step back to enjoy the sparkle!

- Use denture cleanser tablets dissolved in a glass of water to make your diamonds sparkle. Just drop jewelry in the solution for 2 minutes.

- Soak your gems, precious or semiprecious, in a glass of club soda overnight. In the morning, they'll sparkle and shine.

- Does a ring discolor your finger? Apply clear nail enamel to the inside of the band.

- Keep it clean: Prevent your silver jewelry and your costume jewelry from tarnishing by putting a stick of chalk in the jewelry box.

- Does your jewelry box look as if the chains have been wrestling with each other? Solve that problem by dropping each chain through the end of a drinking straw that's been cut in half. Fasten the clasp on the outside of the straw.

- Untangling a fine gold or silver chain can seem hopeless. Try setting the chain on a piece of cling wrap and putting a small drop of baby oil on the knot. Using 2 sewing needles, gently work apart the knot. Wash with water and a little Dawn dishwashing liquid; rinse and dry well.

Beat Spots and Stains

When you walk into some homes, it's like entering an archaeological site: faint crayon marks on the wallpaper record the toddler age, grease spots on the carpet in front of the door to the garage recall the period of do-it-yourself car maintenance, and the discolored spots on the living room carpet will never forget Fido. Most of us don't want our houses to say quite so much about us. We'll help you deal with the unusual and not-so-unusual spots and stains that find their way onto your carpeting, your clothes, your furniture, and the other surfaces in your home. Each stain requires its own special treatment, or you may end up with a worse mess than you started with. We want to share with you some basic information about stains and stain-removal. We'll give you a comprehensive shopping list of cleaning tools and products that you will want to have in your stain-removal kit to combat stains, and we'll teach you the eight basic techniques of stain-removal.

Three Kinds of Stains

Greasy Stains:

You can sometimes remove grease spots from washable fabrics by laundering. Pretreating by rubbing detergent directly into the spot often helps, as does using dry-cleaning solution on the stain. If you are treating an old stain or one that has been ironed, a yellow stain may remain after treatment with a solvent. Bleach can sometimes remove this yellow residue.

To remove grease spots from nonwashable fabrics, sponge the stain with dry-cleaning solution. Elimination of the stain may require several applications. Allow the spot to dry completely between spongings. Greasy stains may also be removed from nonwashable fabrics by using an absorbent, such as cornstarch, cornmeal, French chalk, or fuller's earth (mineral clay available at most drug stores). Dust the absorbent on the greasy spot. When it begins to look caked, it should be shaken or brushed off.

Absorbents are easy to use and will not harm fabrics. However, other stain-removal agents, such as detergents, dry-cleaning solvents, and bleach, can damage fibers. Before using any of these products, you should carefully read the care label on the stained item and the label on the product container. If you do not have either one of these labels, we recommend that you test the cleaning product on the fabric in an inconspicuous area.

Nongreasy Stains:

Fruit juice on your collar, black coffee on your lapel, tea on your pocket flap, food coloring on your cuff, ink on your pant leg— nongreasy stains are easy to acquire, but not impossible to remove. If you are treating a nongreasy stain on a washable fabric, we recommend that you sponge the stain with cool water as soon as possible.

If this doesn't remove the stain, try soaking the fabric in cool water. The stain may soak out within half an hour, or you may need to leave the item in water overnight.

If some of the stain still remains after this treatment, try gently rubbing liquid detergent into it, then rinse with cool water. The very last resort is to use bleach, but always read the fabric-care label before you bleach. If the stain is old or has already been ironed, it may be impossible to remove it completely.

A nongreasy stain on fabric that cannot be washed can be sponged with cool water. Place an absorbent pad under the stained area and slowly drip water through the fabric with an eye dropper or pump/trigger spray bottle. This method of flushing the stain lets you control the amount of water and the rate at which it flows through the fabric so that you don't inadvertently spread the stain.

If you treat a nongreasy stain with water while it is still fresh, you often can remove it entirely. If water alone fails to remove the stain, work liquid detergent into the stain and rinse it by sponging or flushing with cool water. Sponge the spot with rubbing alcohol after you've rinsed it to remove detergent residue and to speed drying. (Caution: If you're treating acetate, acrylic, modacrylic, rayon, triacetate, or vinyl, be sure to dilute the alcohol with water, 1 part alcohol to 2 parts water.)

Combination Stains:

Some stains are double trouble. Coffee with cream, Thousand Island salad dressing, and lipstick leave a trail of combination stains behind them; they're both greasy and nongreasy. Getting rid of combination stains is a two-part operation. First get rid of the nongreasy stain and then attack the greasy residue. On most fabrics, you'll need to sponge the stain with cool water, then work liquid detergent into the stain and rinse thoroughly. After the fabric has dried, apply dry-cleaning solution to the greasy part of the stain. Allow the fabric to dry.

Taking the Stress Out of Stains

There's a surefire strategy for beating stains. You'll save time by doing it right the first time rather than wasting time experimenting with various cures for the problem and possibly making the stain worse than it was to start with.

Here are the basic rules.

- The quicker the better. The best time to treat a stain is the moment after it occurs. The longer it sets, the more likely it is that a stain will become permanent.

- Know what you're cleaning. Identify both the staining agent and the stained surface. Both will affect the way in which you treat the stain.

- Clean it off before you clean it. Remove as much of the staining agent as you possibly can before you begin the stain-removal process.

- Be gentle. Rubbing, folding, wringing, and squeezing cause stains to penetrate more deeply and may damage delicate fibers.

- Keep it cool. Avoid using hot water, high-heat clothes dryers, and irons on stains; heat makes some stains impossible to remove.

- Pretest stain removers. Even clear water can damage some fabrics, so test every cleaner you plan to use in an inconspicuous place before you use it on the stain.

- Follow directions. Read manufacturers' care labels and directions on product containers before you start to clean a stain.

- Work from the edges into the center. You won't spread the stain or leave a ring.

Your Stain-Removal Kit

- To beat stains, you have to be prepared. Your well-stocked stain-removal kit, like a first-aid kit, should be ready to help you handle cleaning emergencies whenever they occur.

- Here are the tools you'll need to have in your kit: clean, white cotton cloths; disposable diapers for absorbing flushed cleaning solutions; white blotting paper; white paper toweling; a spoon, blunt knife, or spatula for scraping; an eyedropper or trigger spray bottle; a small brush; several colorfast weights

- Your kit will also need to include a variety of stain-removal agents. What you need depends on what you are likely to have to clean. You will be able to purchase most of them at your local hardware store, grocery store, or pharmacy.

- **Absorbents** "soak up" grease stains. We consider cornmeal the best absorbent for light colors, and fuller's earth the best for dark colors. Spread the absorbent on the stained areas and allow it to work. As the grease is soaked up, the absorbent material will cake or become gummy. It should then be shaken or brushed off. You should repeat the process until the stain has been removed. This may take as long as eight hours or more.

- **Bleaching Agents, Chlorine:** Commonly used to bleach white cotton, linen, and synthetic fabrics, chlorine bleach is a powerful stain remover, which can weaken fibers if it is allowed to stay on fabric for too long a time. Never use chlorine bleach on silk, wool, or fabrics that are exposed to sunlight, such as curtains. Always test chlorine bleach in an inconspicuous place before bleaching an entire item. Caution: Chlorine bleach is poisonous. If it comes in contact with skin or eyes, it will cause burns and irritation.

- **Bleaching Agents, Color Removers:** Hydrosulfite, the active chemical compound in color removers, lightens the color of fabric before it is redyed a lighter color. This chemical also removes some stains from colorfast fibers. Always pretest color remover. If the product causes a distinct color change instead of fading the fabric, you may be able to restore the original color by rinsing immediately with cool water. If the color fades when color remover is applied, the original color cannot be restored. Color remover should not be used in a metal container. Caution: Color removers are poisonous. Avoid prolonged contact with skin. Observe all precautions on the label.

- **Bleaching Agents, Hydrogen Peroxide:** The 3-percent solution of hydrogen peroxide that is sold as a mild antiseptic is a safe bleach for most fibers. A stronger solution used for lightening hair is too strong to use on fabric and other household surfaces. Buy peroxide in small quantities and store it in a cool, dark place; it loses strength quickly after it is opened and if it is exposed to light.

- **Chemical, Acetic acid:** You can buy acetic acid in a 10-percent solution at pharmacies. White vinegar is a 5-percent acetic acid and can be used as a substitute for the stronger solution. Acetic acid is a clear fluid, used full strength to remove stains on silk and wool. It must be diluted with 2 parts water for use on cotton and linen. (We recommend that you test for colorfastness.) Never use this chemical on acetate. If acetic acid causes a color change, try sponging the affected areas with ammonia; this may restore the color.

- **Chemical, Acetone:** Fingernail-polish remover and household-cement thinner are acetone based, but they should not be substituted for pure acetone because they contain other ingredients that may worsen the stain. You can purchase acetone at pharmacies and paint stores. The colorless liquid smells like peppermint, and it can be used on stains caused by substances such as fingernail polish or household cement. Although acetone will damage neither natural fibers nor most synthetics, it should be tested to make sure that dyed fabrics will not be harmed. Acetone should not be used on fabrics containing acetate; it will dissolve them. Caution: Acetone is flammable and evaporates rapidly, producing toxic fumes. When using acetone, work outside or in a well-ventilated area. Avoid inhaling the fumes. Store acetone in a tightly capped container in a cool place.

- **Chemical, Alcohol:** Isopropyl alcohol in a 70-percent solution is sufficient for most stain-removal jobs that call for alcohol. Stronger, denatured alcohol (90-percent solution) can also be used. Be sure you do not buy alcohol with added color or fragrance. Since alcohol will fade some dyes, we recommend that you test it on the fabric you will be cleaning. Alcohol will damage acetate, triacetate, modacrylic, and acrylic fibers. If you must use it on fibers in the acetate family, dilute the alcohol with 2 parts water. Caution: Alcohol is poisonous and flammable.

- **Chemical, Ammonia:** Use plain household ammonia without added color or fragrance for stain removal. Because ammonia affects some dyes, we recommend that you test it on the stained article. To restore color changed by ammonia, rinse the affected area in water and apply a few drops of white vinegar, then rinse with clear water. Ammonia damages silk and wool; if you must use it on these fibers, dilute it with an equal amount of water and use as sparingly as possible. Caution: Ammonia is poisonous. Avoid inhaling its fumes. It will cause burns or irritation if it comes in contact with skin or eyes.

- **Chemical, Coconut Oil:** You can buy coconut oil in drug and health-food stores. It is used in the preparation of dry spotter that is used to remove many kinds of stains. If you cannot obtain coconut oil, you may substitute mineral oil, which is almost as effective. To make dry spotter, combine 1 part coconut oil and 8 parts liquid dry-cleaning solvent. Store this solution in a tightly capped container to prevent evaporation.

- **Chemical, Glycerine:** Use glycerine in the preparation of wet spotter that is used to remove many kinds of stains. To make wet spotter, mix 1 part glycerine, 1 part white dishwashing detergent, and 8 parts water. Store the solution in a plastic squeeze bottle, and shake well before each use.

- **Chemical, Oxalic Acid:** Effective in treating ink and rust stains, oxalic acid crystals are sold in many pharmacies. The crystals must be dissolved in water (1 tablespoon crystals to 1 cup warm water). Test the solution on a hidden corner of the spotted item before using it on the stain. Moisten the stained area with the solution. Allow it to dry, then reapply. Be sure all traces of the solution are rinsed out. Caution: Oxalic acid is poisonous. Avoid contact with skin and eyes, and wear rubber gloves when working with this chemical.

- **Chemical, Turpentine:** Most often used as a thinner for oil-based paints, turpentine is effective on paint and grease stains. Caution: Turpentine is flammable and poisonous. Observe all the precautions stated on the label.

- **Chemical, Vinegar:** When using vinegar on a stain, always use white (clear) vinegar. Cider and red-wine vinegar have color that can leave a stain. Vinegar is a 5-percent acetic acid solution and should be diluted if you use it on cotton or linen. Vinegar is safe for all other colorfast fibers, but it can change the color of some dyes, so always test it on an inconspicuous area first. If an article changes color, rinse the affected area with water to which you've added a few drops of ammonia. Rinse thoroughly with clear water. This may restore the color.

- **Washing Agents, Detergents:** When stain-removal directions call for a mild detergent, choose a white dishwashing liquid; the dyes in nonwhite detergents may worsen the stain. When instructions call for a pretreating paste made of detergent and water, use a powdered detergent that does not contain bleach. When the stain-removal directions specify that you should apply a liquid laundry detergent directly to the spot or stain, be sure to read the directions on the product's label carefully. Some products cannot safely be used in this manner. Other detergent products, such as those used in automatic dishwashers or for heavy-duty household cleaning, and certain laundry products may contain alkalies. They can set stains caused by ammonia, soap, and oven cleaner and should not be used for spot removal.

- **Washing Agents, Enzyme Presoaks:** Most effective on protein stains, such as those caused by meat juices, eggs, and blood, enzyme presoaks may harm silk and wool. Make sure you have exhausted every alternative before you use enzyme presoaks on these two fabrics. Use a presoak as soon as possible after mixing with water; enzyme-presoak solutions become inactive in storage. Be sure to read and observe all the directions on the product label.

- **Washing Agents, Powdered Cleansers:** Scouring powders and baking soda can be used to remove stains on surfaces that will not be harmed by abrasives. However, you should be aware that prolonged or overly vigorous scrubbing with these products can scratch even the most durable surface. Make sure you rinse away all the powder when the job is completed.

- **Washing Agents, Pretreaters:** Use pretreaters on spots and stains when you think that a stain might not respond to normal laundering procedures. Pretreaters start the cleaning process before the stained item is put in the washer. They must be used in conjunction with the rest of the laundering process; do not try to use a pretreater alone, as though it were a spot remover. After applying a pretreater, you should not allow the fabric to dry out before you begin washing.

- **Washing Agents, Soaps:** Bath soaps with added moisturizers, fragrance, dyes, or deodorant should not be used to treat spots. Purchase either laundry soap or pure white soap.

Safety Precautions

In order to treat stains and spots as soon as they occur, you have to be prepared. But many of the products you stock in your stain-removal kit are flammable or toxic, and certain safety tips should be kept in mind when storing and using these products.

- Store stain-removing products carefully and out of the reach of children. The storage area should be cool, dry, and separate from food storage areas. Keep bottles tightly capped and boxes closed.

- Do not transfer cleaning products to new containers. Keep them in their original containers so that you never have to search for directions for their proper use and so that they are always clearly labeled.

- Follow the directions on the product label and heed all warnings.

- Glass and unchipped porcelain containers are preferable to metal or plastic when working with stain-removal agents. Never use plastic with solvents. Never use any container that is rusty. Clean all containers thoroughly after use.

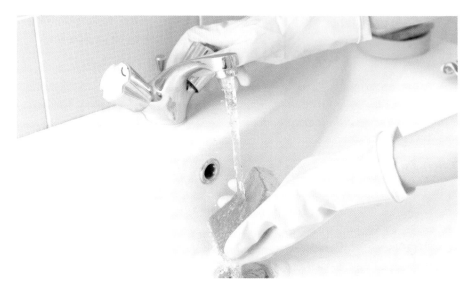

- Protect your hands with rubber gloves. Don't touch your eyes or skin while handling stain-removal chemicals. If you do accidentally touch your eyes or spill chemicals on your skin, flush immediately with clear water.

- Remember that the fumes of solvents are toxic; work in a well-ventilated area.

- Do not use chemicals near an open flame or electrical outlet. Do not smoke while using chemicals.

- Do not use a solvent as a laundry additive.

- When using a solvent on a washable fabric, be sure to rinse all traces of the solvent out of the fabric.

- Do not experiment with mixtures of stain-removal agents. Never combine products unless specifically directed to do so in the recipes for homemade cleaning solutions in this book. Many combinations can be dangerous.

- If the cleaning process requires the use of more than one stain-removal agent, rinse out each product thoroughly before applying the next.

Eight Ways to Beat Stains

We would all like to be able to squirt a little dab of the right solution on a stain, stand back, and watch the spot fade away forever. Unfortunately, stain removal has not yet become quite that simple. But can beat the stain with a combination of the right techniques and the right cleaning solutions.

We have already discussed the cleaning supplies you need to have on hand in your stain-removal kit, but you also need to know how these tools and products are used to remove stains quickly and effectively.

There are eight basic techniques for stain removal: brushing, flushing, freezing, presoaking, pretreating, scraping, sponging, and tamping. The right technique for a particular spot or stain depends on what was spilled and where it fell.

Use **brushing** to remove dried stains. Some kinds of spots, such as dried mud, can be removed completely by brushing. For other kinds of stains, brushing is only a step in the cleaning process.

We recommend a small, stiff-bristled brush for this technique. When you're working on fabric, stretch the piece on a firm, clean surface. Hold a sheet of paper next to the stain, and brush the staining material onto the paper. A gentle motion with the brush pulls the stain up off the surface and onto the paper.

Use **flushing** to remove loosened staining materials and the residue from stain-removal agents. If cleaning products are left in the material, they may cause additional staining or even damage the treated article.

When you are flushing a stain, especially one on nonwashable fabric, you need to control the flow of water carefully so that you don't spread the stain or get the fabric wetter than you need to. An eyedropper or a trigger spray bottle that can be adjusted to a fine stream lets you precisely control the amount of liquid flushed through the fabric. Before you begin this treatment, place a clean absorbent pad, such as a disposable diaper, under the spot. Then slowly and carefully apply water or the recommended stain remover to the stain. Work slowly so that you don't flood the pad with more liquid than it can absorb. Replace the absorbent pad frequently to prevent the deposited staining material from restaining the fabric. If you're treating a stain on a washable fabric, rinse the article in warm water after you have flushed the stain.

Candle wax, chewing gum, and other gooey substances are easier to remove when they are cold and hard. Hold an ice cube against the stain to **freeze** it. If the stained item is not washable, place the ice in a plastic bag. You can put a small stained item in a plastic bag and place the whole thing in the freezer. After the stain has solidified, it can usually be gently lifted or scraped from the surface.

When your wash is grayed, yellowed, or heavily soiled, washing alone will not get it clean and bright— you will have to **presoak**. Sort the soiled items before presoaking; items that are not colorfast should be presoaked separately from colorfast items because their colors may bleed.

You may add bleach, laundry detergent, or an enzyme presoak to the soaking water. But don't use chlorine bleach and an enzyme product at the same time. You can leave colorfast, stained articles in a presoak for as long as it takes to get them clean, but for most stains, 30 minutes is long enough. Items that aren't colorfast should be soaked only briefly.

Before you wash a load of presoaked laundry, make sure that it has been thoroughly rinsed and that no residue of the presoak is left on the items.

Pretreat oily, greasy stains with liquid laundry detergent, a soil-and-spot-removing spray, bar soap, or a pretreating paste made from powdered detergent and water. After you apply a pretreater, rub it into the stain gently, and wash the item as you would normally.

Scrape away solid staining material with a dull knife, spoon, or spatula before you apply stain remover. Don't press too hard; move the edge of your scraping tool back and forth across the stain in short strokes.

Put an absorbent pad, such as a disposable diaper, under the stain before you **sponge** it. On a carpet you will have to work without an absorbent pad, so be especially careful not to use excessive amounts of cleaning solution or water. Use another pad or a sponge to apply the stain-removing agent.

Sponge the stain gently using light strokes. Change either pad as soon as any of the stain is deposited on it.

Some fabrics, such as acetate, triacetate, and rayon, are likely to develop rings when they are sponged. When you work on stains on these fabrics, barely wet the pad with stain remover and touch the fabric lightly so that the stain remover is absorbed as slowly as possible. Blot the treated area between absorbent pads. Allow it to air-dry. Ironing or drying with heat may cause the stain remover itself to stain the fabric.

The best way to get some stains out of durable, tightly woven fabrics is to **tamp** them with a soft-bristled brush. Place the stained article on a hard work surface, not on a pad, and lightly rap the stain with the tips of the bristles. Repeat until the stain is removed. Use this technique rarely, because tamping will harm most fabrics.